ANCIENT ENGLAND

ANCIENT ENGLAND

NIGEL BLUNDELL & KATE FARRINGTON

PROSPERO B·O·O·K·S

A DIVISION OF CHAPTERS INC.

ACKNOWLEDGMENTS

The publishers and the authors would like to thank in particular English Heritage who provided the bulk of the photographs, Historic Scotland for the photograph on page 51 and Garry Gibbons for those on pages 63(B), 66, 74/5, 76/7, 85(T), 88(T), 92(Both), 94/5, 97, 111, 137(T), 138(T), 139, 140/1, 144

Photograph Page 1: *Castle Rigg stone circle.*

Photograph Page 2: *Belsay Hall, castle and gardens.*

This edition first published in 1996 by the
Promotional Reprint Company Ltd,
Kiln House,
210 New Kings Road,
London SW6 4NZ.

This edition produced in 1999 for Prospero Books,
A division of Chapters Inc.

ISBN 1 55267 993 4

Printed and bound in China

CONTENTS

INTRODUCTION

The creation of Britain's landscape as we know it today is a diverse and dramatic story. As in every awesome history, it is people and their lives over thousands of years who shape their environment and leave their mark on every fibre of their country for generations of their ancestors to discover and marvel upon.

Such a series of transient presences — from the time humans made their first appearance there three million years ago, through the ensuing waves of their migrating successors until the 20th century Englishman and woman — cannot be without its mystery and magic. Ancient sites still survive, ancient stones still stand and ancient signs still exist of those who walked these shores and thus designed its land and culture. We can sometimes only surmise the purpose of these treasures unintentionally bequeathed to us.

Yet much of England's intriguing canvas of changing colours, contours and scenes was determined millions of years before man's intervention. The band of limestone running from Devonshire, Dorset and Somerset through the Cotswolds, Oxfordshire and on to the North Yorkshire moors, for example, was formed 200 million years ago beneath the waters of tropical seas. The downlands of southern England are all that remain of the Great Chalk Sea which covered most of Europe 100 million years later. Countless layers of tiny, single-cell creatures collected on the sea-bed at the rate of one metre every 100,000 years. The carpet of white chalk is 500 metres (approximately 1,500 ft) thick in places.

Some 18,000 million years ago all of 'Britain' down to South Wales and the Wash lay under an ice sheet, which was up to a mile thick in places. This was the Fourth Ice Age, the last in a series of glaciations which peaked every 100,000 years. South of the ice line lay a vast area of arctic tundra, extending down as far as Bordeaux in south-west France. Beneath the ice, valleys were gouged out in the mountains of Snowdonia, whilst the hills of north England were ground smooth where the rocks were soft, or carved into jagged peaks if they were hard. Between these four Ice Ages, a new species crept across the harsh landscape — humans.

Palaeolithic (Old Stone Age) Man had arrived across the land-bridge which linked 'Britain' with the rest of the continent. Little is known of those very early peoples and the methods they used to forge a living from their surroundings, as most traces of them have been obscured by the effects of time and obliterated by the great glacial grindings and upheavals.

Human progress from the end of the last Ice Age presents a clearer picture. From, around 10,000BC, man, armed with weapons fashioned from stone, stalked the migrating herds of mammoths, woolly rhinoceros and reindeer which grazed the Eurasian plains. As he became more sophisticated, he hunted many of these larger beasts to extinction. With the reduction of the plant-rich tundra, other species disappeared — leaving the two-legged human as master of the bleak lands he surveyed.

THE AGES OF PREHISTORY

Scholars divide the long span of prehistory into several ages. These dates, although only approximate, are commonly accepted divisions for the prehistory of England:

Palaeolithic or Old Stone Age:	300,000 to 8000BC
Mesolithic or Middle Stone Age:	8000 to 2700BC
Neolithic or New Stone Age:	2700 to 1900BC
Bronze Age:	1900 to 500BC
Iron Age:	500 BC to 51BC★

★51BC was the date of publication of Julius Caesar's *Gallic Wars* and the beginning of fully recorded history in North-western Europe.

Right: *Perhaps the most potent symbol of English nationality is the country's patron saint, St George. This wall painting, at Pickering Parish Church, shows him saving a maiden from a dragon a legend that seems to be based on adventures of the winged horse, Pegasus, in Greek mythology. The cult of St George emerged strongly in England after it was spread by Crusaders returning from the Middle East.*

THE MAKING OF AN ISLAND RACE

It was 8,500 years ago that the remaining glaciers of the last Ice Age finally melted and swelled the grey, gloomy sea waters to an unprecedented level. Slowly, as if aware of the historic waves it was making, the sea swamped miles of marsh lands. Thus, around 6500BC, Britain became an island.

That enforced isolation created a fresh canvas, upon which the only marks were the rudimentary settlements and tracks left by the mysterious, vanished Palaeolithic (Old Stone Age) Man. Now, with the hairy Ice Age beasts replaced by the bear, boar and wolf, the most primitive inhabitants of this land were also supplanted, by Mesolithic (Middle Stone Age) Man.

Now that the lumbering, large beasts had been eradicated, new sources of food had to be found and new ways of securing it developed. The human hunters learned to give the wild animals the chance to breed, instead of immediately slaughtering any edible creature they encountered. It made good sense for communities to have charge of their own wild herds. People discovered, too, that cereals and berries grew more plentiful on countryside cleared of dense woodland. Both newly-found ways of ensuring continued food supplies were the ancient basis for today's farming practices.

Other early inhabitants soon realised that the very sea which had cast them adrift from the rest of the world could be their friend too. Existence relied on regular fish harvests and campsites in the most prolific areas were soon set up. These included what is today the lower Bann Valley in and around Lough Neagh, in the north-east of Ireland, and the beaches of modern day Devon and Dorset, where an abundance of crab, limpet, whelks, oysters and lobsters provided a varied diet.

Up until this time, the human population of England probably numbered only a few thousand. Then came a 'population explosion'. From 5000BC, Neolithic (New Stone Age) Man began arriving from the Mediterranean. These accomplished sailors and traders came in boats laden with wheat, barley and domesticated animals. They were organised farmers and undertook extensive deforestation. Their knowledge of grain growing, animal husbandry and agriculture set in motion a social revolution and their numbers grew to between 30,000 and 50,000.

This more civilised approach to living was followed in turn by greater respect of the dead — for the ancestors. Neolithic man made his mark on the landscape with great ritual monuments, venerating his dead and marking the cycles of the seasons. Up to 4400BC, bodies had been simply covered in earth. Now, following continental burial procedures, tombs which were designed to hold several bodies were built.

There were two main types of tomb: the chambered tomb, usually a rectangular box of large rock slabs (of which remains still stand at Waylands Smith in Berkshire) and a similar structure made of

Above: *An artist's impression of a thanksgiving ceremony at Grimes Graves, a massive network of Neolithic flint mines in Norfolk.*

wood, built in areas where rock was scarce (such at at Fussell's Lodge in Wiltshire). Other larger burial sites (including Hambledon Hill in Dorset and Hazelton in Gloucestershire) were later established, the dead only being laid to rest after increasingly elaborate rituals.

Britain's landscape was now visibly changing. Two thousand years of relatively stable climate resulted in the isles being covered by broadleaf woodland. Only the highest mountains, the extreme north and the coastal dunes and marshes lacked a rich and varied range of trees.

The first trees to return after the ice were those which could survive in colder climates, such as birch, sallow and aspen. Then, over a period of several thousand years, warmer climate trees began to grow, including pine, alder, hazel and the mighty English oak. It was within these woods that settlers made bases for hunting and gathering food. These settlements had skin tents with sunken floors to give proper shelter. Sites such as those discovered at Church Hill,

Findon, West Sussex, were excavated on a massive scale to gather flint for making hunting weapons and tools. Hard rock, as found at Cornwall's Lizard Peninsula, was used for making axes not only for hunting but as 'money' — exchanging the weapons for cattle and other goods. Another remote site, the Pike of Stickle summit, at the head of Langdale Valley in the Lake District, still shows indentations created by axe makers who were prepared to risk their lives for stones they believed had magical powers.

Working the land, crop growing and eating habits continued to undergo changes as the people grew more sophisticated and knowledgeable about their lands. Ploughs and draught animals were employed, taking over from simple crop cultivation using sticks. Large areas of forests were being cleared to provide greater areas for crops and herds. Farming became established as the key to prosperity and social standing, so certain cattle herders began to control neighbouring groups or tribes. These tribal leaders established ringed enclosures, such as Hambledon Hill in Dorset and Crickley Hill in Gloucestershire. Fierce rivalry broke out and settlements deemed too rich were attacked.

The diet of the native Englishman became more varied. Evidence at sites such as Runnymede, Surrey, proves that clay pots were used for storage and as cooking vessels — the latter, by 4100BC, were used for the recently introduced continental dishes of stews and casseroles.

It was in these changing, often violent times, that perhaps England's most magical, most mystical of landmarks were created. They are what is known as 'henges', large, circular monuments developed from old enclosures, ringed with ditches. One particular site —Stonehenge in Wiltshire — is on an astonishing scale. In the following chapter we will explore its magic further. Suffice it to say here that modern Britons, while marvelling at the monumental scale

of the ancient site, can only guess at why and just how those massive stones could have been put in place by an apparently primitive people, who at that stage had not even discovered the wheel.

It is believed that these henges were used for communal ritual. The new gods were the sun, the moon and the earth, and worship was undertaken with the accent on death being shut out from these temples. This makes sense, for by now death was no longer revered but instead feared. This fear saw communal burial places and tombs sealed off to make death, quite simply, disappear from sight. Gigantic rocks still exist at West Kennet, Avebury, in Wiltshire, 'barring' the way to tomb chambers. People no longer worshiped their ancestors in tombs filled with skulls. Similar henges were constructed at Duggleby Howe, North Yorkshire, and at Shepperton in Surrey.

Not all henges were man-made, however. Today there still exists at Castlerigg, overlooking Derwent Water in Cumbria, an imposing circle of stones left behind by the glaciers all those thousands of years ago.

What kind of people worshiped at these places? Britain was no longer home only to the ancient British migratory races who had settled there in prehistoric times. As the populations in such far-off lands as Assyria and Mesopotamia grew and land became over-

farmed to feed hungry mouths, these peoples left their native sur-
rounds. Over generations, by taking tortuous routes toward the
Mediterranean basin, up the Danube valley and across central
Europe to the shore of the Baltic and on to the North Sea, they
finally found their new home in Britain.

The tiny British Isles became haven to bands of immigrant farmers whose techniques were to shape the country's agriculture.
Something else was becoming vital to the life of ancient Britain
around 2000BC; a new type of metal had been discovered —
bronze.

Top Left: *A typical family group gathered beside a river at Boxgrove flint quarry, a
Palaeolithic site near Chichester.*

Left: *An artist's impression of how Boxgrove Man might have looked.*

Far Left: *A reconstruction of a gathering at Avebury, one of Europe's greatest stone
circles and a key religious site in the west of England. Avebury comprises two
separate circles, totalling some 60 stones, with a further 100 forming a larger,
irregular ring.*

Above and Right: *The stones at Avebury are thought to have been raised around
2500BC.*

Castle Rigg, northern England's most impressive stone circle, stands below the snow-capped peaks of Cumbria. Legend has it that the stones can never be properly counted.

Left: *A closer view of Castle Rigg's stones. The circle has a rough diameter of 34m (111ft) and contains a rectangular stone setting on its south-east side.*

Top: *The purpose of Silbury Hill, the largest man-made mound in Europe, is still a mystery. It is founded on a natural chalk spur and was built up to 40m (130ft) by a series of stepped layers. Carbon dating for the first phase suggests work began at around the same time as Avebury.*

Above: *The Belas Knapp long barrow in Gloucestershire; a later Neolithic style of burial, with graves set into the sides, as well as the centre, of the mound.*

Right: *An artist's impression showing the huge labour force needed for the construction of Silbury.*

THE MYSTERY OF STONEHENGE

Few relics of the ancient world are as mystifying as the great standing pillars of Stonehenge. These megaliths of ancient man defy belief: how did they get there, what is their purpose, where did the technology to erect them come from?

Across the centuries, the giant, brooding stones of this awe-inspiring ruin have stood as a challenge to man's knowledge of himself and his ancient world. But despite every theory, they still keep their secrets. For they are made from rocks only found hundreds of miles from Stonehenge. How were the stones transported? How was this miracle of engineering performed? And above all, why?

Stonehenge, however, is but one cluster in a swathe of gigantic monumental rocks which stretches around Europe and the British Isles, from as far north as the Shetland Islands to Malta in the south. There are around 900 sites of standing stones in Britain alone. But Stonehenge, rising above the flat plateau of Salisbury Plain, is easily the most famous of them. Indeed, among all the great stone sites of Europe, Stonehenge remains unique because of the sophisticated way that the blocks appear to have been designed to fit one another and to form a carefully complete whole.

It is only relatively recently that archaeologists have been prepared to say that these great stones may have been the work of advanced astronomers or mathematicians rather than barbarians and savages. Astute detective work has resulted in extraordinary theories on the history of the megaliths (the word is Greek for 'great stones') which should not be dismissed lightly.

The site of Stonehenge was a prehistoric sanctuary in use from circa 3100 to 1100BC. The temple itself was built in three distinct stages, spanning a period of over 1,000 years. Each group of people who began the mammoth task did not quite finish it, leaving the legacy of completion to the succeeding generations.

The first builders were Neolithic, working on the site around 2700BC. It was they who set up the encircling ditch and bank and the heel stone, which is aligned so that the first rays of light from the sun on midsummer's day strike both it and the central point of the two stone circles. These same people created the 56 shallow pits called the Aubrey Holes — named after the writer who discovered them — which form a ring just inside the bank, and which when excavated were found to contain bones and cremated objects.

Some 800 years on, the men and women whom we call the Beaker People moved in on the site. They, by means unknown, accomplished one of the truly great engineering feats of all time. In an age when tools were of flint and bone and the wheel had not been invented, they hewed rock from the Prescelly Hills in South Wales and carried it the 480 kilometres (300 miles) to Stonehenge. The 80 mammoth bluestones, each weighing more than 4,000kg (4 tons), were then assembled into a double circle inside the earlier enclosure.

Above and Right: *Stonehenge remains one of ancient England's most enduring and intriguing mysteries. Evidence increasingly points to its use as an early astronomical observatory and the sheer extravagance of the design implies that the site was of major social and religious significance.*

Around 1500BC, the builders of the third Stonehenge again brought in massive boulders, this time from the Marlborough Downs, probably dragged to the site on primitive sledges by upwards of 1,000 men. The individual boulders weighed more than 51,000kg (50 tons) each, and were hewn from sarsen rock, one of the hardest minerals found in these islands. After the arduous journey, they were fashioned into the shapes which now stand like gaunt sentinels on the bleak, windswept plain.

Finally, a people who could not read or write or fashion a wheel devised a system to put the huge stone lintels on top of the upright stones. In addition, Stonehenge man shared something with the prehistoric builders at other sites around Europe — all these monuments are constructed using the same unit of measurement, a unit archaeologists have come to call the 'megalithic yard': a distance of 0.83 metres (0.9 yds). No one has yet been able to explain either how or why this common unit could have come to be used so widely by so many distant peoples at the time.

Although the strange cult of the modern Druids, or Celtic Priests, now lays claim to Stonehenge, experts concur that it is far too old to have been constructed by their Celtic forerunners. So which cult and which people were behind the megalithic mystery?

Theories about the structure abound, but perhaps the following bears the greatest credence. In 1934, after a hard day's sailing, Professor Alexander Thom, of Oxford University, took his boat into Loch Roag on the Isle of Lewis, off Scotland's bleak west coast. Silhouetted against the rising full moon were the standing stones of Callanish, Scotland's own 'Stonehenge'. The professor went ashore. Standing in the middle of the stone circle, he checked the position of the Pole Star and noted that it showed the structure was aligned due north-south. Because this monument was prehistoric and was built in the days when the Pole Star's constellation had not reached its present position in the sky, Professor Thom deduced that the people who had built it must have had some other way of determining the alignment of the stones.

His discovery there launched him on a quest around 600 standing stone sites both in Britain and Europe. He proved that although the stone circles may look rough and weathered today, worn down by both time and human activities, they were originally precise works of engineering skill. Of Stonehenge, he declared that it was a Stone Age observatory, where even small irregularities on the extremities of the site were created artificially, specifically to mark the significant moments when the sun and moon rose and set.

In 1963 studies at Boston University revealed that Stonehenge was like a giant computer: a huge observatory capable of extreme-ly complex calculations based on the sun, moon and stars. When all the data about the site was fed into a computer, the startling result was that the stones could be used to predict the occurrence of eclipses. It seemed that the highly educated astronomer priests of the time could have stood in the centre of the great circle and determined the position of the sun or moon in its orbit by using the stones as a guide.

Such sophistication among the ancients seemed at first difficult to accept; yet the men who built Stonehenge had proved by the feat itself that they were not primitive. It has even been claimed that these people had established an elite 'academy' where the most gifted priests may have lived and studied their craft. Remains found at Durrington Walls, near Stonehenge, reveal a race of people who ate a rich diet, who wore woven cloth and who enjoyed a status above that of their nearest neighbours.

If the academics are right, that Stonehenge and the other standing stone sites were indeed designed for making astronomical observations, it is likely that there was an intellectual elite within the primitive Stone Age farmers we know inhabited the earth — an elite who carried out the complex calculations necessary to chart planetary movements in an age when there was no written word.

Other theories about Stonehenge exist — that the site was a temple for human sacrifice, a place where infertile women went to be blessed by the gods, even that it was a beacon for beings from outer space. It has even been suggested that Stonehenge had a much broader purpose. Charts point to the strange geometric pattern that exists between Stonehenge, the prehistoric hill site nearby called Old Sarum, and another Neolithic settlement called Grovelly Castle. The three sites are 9.6 kilometres (0.6 miles) from each other, so that when joined on a map a near-perfect equilateral triangle emerges; was this town planning on a huge and precise scale, or merely coincidence?

Despite these diverse propositions, the observatory theory stands best the test of time. And scientists now accept the once unbelievable proposition that a phenomenally intellectual race long ago learned to operate a gigantic stone 'computer'…

Below: *A bird's eye view of Old Sarum, near Salisbury, Wiltshire, as it is today and* **(Above Right)** *as it would have appeared in the middle of the 12th century. Some of the original stonework, like that at Bishop Roger's Palace* **(Below Right)***, is still in place.*

OLD SARUM

Old Sarum is a ghost town, probably the finest example in England of an entire city deserted at the height of its development. People lived on the site for more than 4,000 years, ever since it was first occupied by Iron Age tribesmen. They were followed in turn by Romans, Saxons and Normans, who built a castle, cathedral and two royal palaces. However, when a new cathedral was built at New Sarum, or Salisbury, in the 13th century, the old city quickly declined. Today all that remains are 227 square meters (56 acres), including the earthworks and 202 square meters (50 acres) of ruins that create an eerie reminder of tribal life in England five millennia ago.

AGES OF BRONZE
AND IRON

The practice of burial and religious ritual flourished with the arrival of the Beaker People from their homelands on the Rhine around 2000BC. Indeed, their name is derived from their habit of burying ornate pottery artifacts which were discovered inside their burial mounds. The Beaker People also brought with them skills in working bronze, a mixture of copper with a little tin. Their ability to work metal and make tools led to more sophisticated methods of cultivation which resulted in turn in a population explosion. Over a few hundred years, the number of people in Britain rose to about one million. Settlements flourished as did fortified hilltop villages, each linked by a network of tracks. Large systems of cultivated fields appeared, covering thousands of acres. This signified the start of the deliberate sculpting of the British landscape which would continue through four millennia.

But what sort of people were these Bronze Age Britons? How did they get here and how harsh was their existence once they had arrived? The greatest clue came only in the last decade of the 20th century — with the discovery of a single wooden boat...

The so-called Bronze Age Boat was a history-shattering archaeological discovery made on the site of a later Roman harbour wall during road-widening work in Dover, Kent, in 1992. About 7 metres (20 ft) down was a largely intact, plank-sewn boat, some 18 metres long by 3 metres wide (60 by 10ft). Beautifully built, it was a sophisticated piece of marine engineering crafted 3,500 years ago.

Today crossing the 35 kilometres (22 miles) of sea between Britain and France is plain sailing. But in prehistoric times, the adventures of the motley crews who manned Dover's Bronze Age Boat touched on the miraculous. They journeyed in what was little more than tree trunks, with oxen and sheep jostling at their elbows and with water lapping at their ankles. It would have taken around eight hours for Bronze Age Man to cross the short stretch of sea at about six knots, with up to 24 paddlers stopping every so often to bail out.

There being no nails or glue in those days, the Dover Bronze Age Boat was made up of just six timbers from three giant oak trees. Saws had not been invented either but the timbers had been hewn and split with absolute precision, using bronze axes, gouges, chisels and even flint tools. They were then lashed together with 'rope' made from flexible yew stems. Moss, used to fill gaps left between rope and wood, was still growing. Pieces of French pottery were found in the boat, proving that it was, in effect, an 'international ferry'. Odd items used for plugging leaky holes were also still in place; somebody's underpants or shirt tail has been ripped off to caulk one of these holes because it has sprung a leak at sea.

With a date of 1500BC, the Bronze Age Boat is therefore the oldest craft in Europe and the third oldest in the world — beaten only by two ancient Egyptian boats. That means that as masons were putting their finishing touches to Stonehenge, accomplished seamen were already operating the first-ever ferry between the har-

Above: *The Cerne Abbas giant in Dorset is cut into a chalk hillside. It has been an unmistakable fertility symbol for centuries.*

Right: *An artist's impression of a couple of remote Bronze Age huts as they would have appeared in the rugged country of Brean Down, a narrow headland near Weston-super-Mare, Avon.*

bours of what were to become Dover and Calais. The boat's remarkably preserved state was due to it being encased in sediment laid down during a rise in sea level after the Bronze Age. Also encased in the mud were fragments which did not come from the craft. They weren't fully worked, suggesting that the site was where boats were manufactured or repaired — in other words a boat yard.

Dover's Bronze Age gem has given us the most amazing insight into Britain's past since modern man first marvelled at Stonehenge. For Dover, known through recent history as the 'Key To England', is now known to have been exactly that an amazing 3,500 years ago. And Kent is now known to have been a bustling trading region ... at a time when it was believed Ancient Britons could not even build ships!

Thus we know of a sophistication hitherto undreamed of in an age of prehistory which has left us no language, no literature and,

apart from the henges, few structures on the landscape. Until recent years it was thought that England at this time was submerged in a series of barbaric invasions from the continent. In fact, the Bronze Age history of England was probably a series of many native-born developments. Not only is continental pottery found in England but English pottery is found on the continent. There was a large-scale trade in metals, the main market for British bronze being to Scandinavia. English farmers were wealthy enough to bury their dead with gold, amber and even beads from the Orient.

Having developed the ox-drawn plough, agriculture flourished to an unprecedented degree. Farms, with dwelling sites, on a large scale are still evident on the untrammelled heaths of Dartmoor and the moors of North Yorkshire. More prominent are the 'barrows', or circular burial mounds, of the Sussex Downs, Salisbury Plain, the Derbyshire Peak District and the Yorkshire Wold.

From this evidence we know that England was populated by a stable, industrious peasant population, living by agriculture and the keeping of livestock, as well as by hunting and fishing. They lived in hut villages along riverbanks or in isolated farms on the chalk downs or upland moors, largely cleared of native forest and scrub. There was little sign of fortification. Which means that Bronze Age Man was totally unprepared for the next period in the history of ancient England: the Age Of Iron.

Although bronze implements remained in use, particularly in northern Britain, until the last century before Christ, iron was a stronger material for both sword and plough share. First dug and forged on the continent, iron was brought to England in a fresh series of invasions — by a people whose origins remain mysterious.

From the styles of their weapons and drinking cups, it is sur-

mised that the early Iron Age invaders emanated from as far afield as Austria and Switzerland. Archaeologists have no clues as to their languages or even the names they used for themselves. It was only when Greek explorers and Roman conquerors came to these northern shores in the late Iron Age that the inhabitants of France and Britain were uniformly labelled 'Gauls' or 'Celts'. But it is a mistake to think that the Celts were a single race with a common culture. The present-day people of Scotland, Ireland, Wales, Cornwall and Brittany, who term themselves 'Celtic', are simply the independently spirited survivors who were squeezed to the edges of the known world upon the decline of Rome.

But Rome's fall was still 1,000 years away as, in around 700BC, the iron-based culture of the Celts first began to spread towards Britain.

Nearly all Iron Age people lived in villages among fields, on river gravels or light upland soils. These stable settlements came about with the establishment of a new farming procedure, repeatedly harvesting, ploughing and resowing their fields. Most villagers depended on a variety of grain as their staple diet and stored it in underground pits. Managed stock-breeding created new, healthy breeds of oxen, pigs, sheep and cattle. Houses were built of wood and wickerwork and coated in mud to weatherproof them. Food was stored, cooked and served in pottery vessels.

Iron Age Society might sound quite civilised but it was, in fact, a violent, often barbaric era. Noblemen of the time won praise for raids, duels and war. Human heads, severed in battle, were said to hold magical powers and were often used in rituals to the gods. Such places as Wookey Hole, in the Mendip Hills of Somerset, were the site of vast stashes of heads and skulls.

As the Iron Age settlements increased, so too did the fighting, sometimes provoked by scarcity of good farming land. A tribal system developed and with it tribal wars. As villages became more prosperous, everyone had more to defend. Huge hilltop forts and camps began to spring up; these consisted of a single rampart, sometimes of stone, but usually an earthwork riveted with timber and

protected by a ditch. Some forts contained 50 houses or more, complete with grain stores, and could sustain around 200 people. One massive construction was at Danebury, near Andover, Hampshire.

In the latter years of the Iron Age, one tribe of immigrating Celts — the Belgae from northern Gaul — spread over Essex, Hertfordshire, and parts of Oxfordshire. Their settlements then began to cover Hampshire, Wiltshire, Dorset and part of Sussex. These new settlers preferred living in towns in valleys, and they established themselves as the elite tribes of Britain as they spread across increasing areas of the country. They built new towns on sites they claimed, including Wheathampstead, Verulamium (St Albans), Camulodunum (Colchester), Calleva (Silchester) and Venta Belgarum (Winchester). These later Iron Age people were also the first to introduce coinage of silver and copper.

The Gallic Celts, being ferocious fighters, tore down many of the 2,000 hill forts that still existed on the British landscape and made the sites their new homes. The Belgae might have acted differently had they known what was about to descend upon them. But then, nothing and no one could have withstood the approaching legions of Rome.

Below: *How the Bronze Age village at Grimspound, on top of Dartmoor in Devon, might have looked. The cattle and sheep in the foreground would have been regarded as a measure of the settlement's prosperity.*

Above Left: *A view of the Carn Euny ancient village in Cornwall, where stone huts replaced timber in the first century BC. This Celtic village includes a fogou — an underground chamber for which the purpose is not known.*

Below Left: *A general view of Grimspound today. There are still the remains of 24 huts and an example of a fine granite slab entrance on the south side.*

Above: *The Ridgeway near Uffington Castle on the Berkshire Downs. Nearby the famous white horse is carved into a hillside.*

Left: *A reconstruction of a typical gathering at Danebury Hill Fort in Hampshire. Excavations suggest that by the time of the Roman invasion Danebury was a sophisticated settlement with carefully planned 'streets'.*

Above Right: *Iron age fortifications still survive at Stanwick, in Northamptonshire.*

Far Right: *An artist's impression of a battle scene at Danebury around 100BC. Iron age forts such as this one seem to have been more-or-less continually occupied over many centuries. In times of war between Celtic chieftains they were seen as a safe refuge for families in otherwise exposed farming settlements.*

Right: *The stone cist at Drixxlecombe.*

VENI, VIDI, VICI

Only now are we about to enter the period of recorded history. This is what an ambitious Roman general, one Julius Caesar, wrote about the unknown island across the water … towards which he was now turning greedy eyes.

'The interior of Britain is inhabited by people who claim, on the strength of an oral tradition, to be aboriginal; the coast by Belgic immigrants who came to plunder and make war — nearly all of them retaining the names of the tribes from which they originated — and later settled down to till the soil. The population is exceedingly large (in fact, probably a little over a million), the ground thickly studded with homesteads, closely resembling those of the Gauls, and the cattle very numerous.

'For money they use either bronze or gold coins or iron ingots of fixed weights. Tin is found inland and small quantities of iron near the coast; the copper that they use is imported. There is timber of every kind, as in Gaul, except beech and fir. Hares, fowl and geese they think it unlawful to eat, but rear them for pleasure and amusement. The climate is more temperate than in Gaul, the cold being less severe.

'By far the most civilised inhabitants are those living in Kent, a purely maritime district, whose way of life differs little from that of the Gauls. Most of the tribes in the interior do not grow corn, but live on milk and meat and wear skins. All the Britons dye their bodies with woad, which produces a blue colour and gives them a more terrifying appearance in battle. They wear their hair long and shave the whole of their bodies except the head and upper lip.

'Wives are shared between groups of 10 or 12 men, especially between brothers and between fathers and sons. But the offspring of these unions are counted as the children of the man with whom a particular woman cohabited first.'

This was how Caesar saw Britain, forming his opinions from the reports of traders. He viewed them as barbarians. And indeed they were, in one particular custom: human sacrifice. The Celts of Iron Age Britain used it to appease the hundreds of gods whom they worshiped. The sheer numbers of gods sealed the fates of criminals and innocents alike.

Caesar further noted of the Celts:

'They believe that the execution of those who have been caught in the act of theft or robbery or some crime is more pleasing to the immortal gods but when the supply of such fails they resort to the execution even of the innocent.'

Roman and Greek writers were genuinely appalled at the barbarity of the Celts even though their own cultures had bloody ceremonies. Elaborating on the ritual of Celtic sacrifices, the contemporary Greek writer and geographer Strabo wrote: 'They would strike the condemned man in the back with a sword and then divine from his death struggle.' In other words, they would 'read' the future from the manner of his death throes — before minutely examining his entrails for further omens.

Alternatively, the Celts might shoot the victims with arrows or impale them at the chosen holy site. Most horrific, however, was the fate of those victims who were crammed dozens at a time into giant wicker cages fashioned in the form of a god and then burned to death. In attendance at such rituals were the Druids, the band of priests and soothsayers whose bloodletting swept France, Britain and Ireland at the time.

Celtic shrines have been unearthed to reveal quantities of human bones, alongside the bones of animals and of tools which have been ritually smashed, all believed to have been gifts to the gods. The Celts are known to have placed such relics in deep shafts — dug, it is believed, in an attempt to communicate with the underworld.

Yet the Celts who lived in late Iron Age England were clearly far from being mere savages, even if the nature of their society was very different from that of Rome. They lacked a developed urban civilisation, a sophisticated system of government with clearly differentiated administrative functions, a permanent army or a literary culture. And, of course, their sacrificial rituals were wholly alien to the more advanced culture of Rome.

But being different is not the same as being primitive. Agriculture was both varied and extensive; arable and pastoral farming were practiced, much of the woodland had been cleared, and ploughs with 'mould-boards' were used to scrape the surface of the earth in readiness for planting crops.

A high and increasing level of settled population was supported and the surplus helped to sustain an aristocratic society. In southern Britain, Celtic 'states' had developed with monarchical patterns of government. The beginnings of towns were to be seen both in the hill forts and in low-lying centres such as Camulodunum (Colchester), capital of the Trinovantes of Essex.

But Britain was not a nation. Not even the southern part of it, which later became England, was in any sense one country. England was first united as a result of conquest – conquest by the most powerful and extensive empire in the history of Europe, that of Rome.

It was in the summer of the Roman year 699, now described as the year 55BC, that the Proconsul of Gaul, Gaius Julius Caesar first set his sights on Britain. The island both fascinated and troubled him, for he well knew it was home to tribesmen similar to those who had confronted the Romans in campaigns in Germany, Spain and Gaul. He also knew the 'islanders' had helped the local tribes in the late campaigns along the northern coast of Gaul. British volunteers had shared the defeat of the Veneti on the coasts of Brittany in the previous year. Furthermore refugees from conquered Gaul were welcomed and sheltered on the island.

Caesar had gleaned further knowledge about this intimidating place called Britannia and was already contemplating putting the island's uneducated, uncouth inhabitants to work as his slaves. The land was green and fertile from which many farming riches could be reaped. He had even heard talk of a pearl fishery and of the presence of gold.

In short, it was time for him to see Britannia for himself. This was no small decision for Caesar to make for the Romans hated and feared the sea. But these feelings were overruled by Caesar's desire to land on such a mysterious and remote island and thereby win great acclaim from all of Roman society. His boast from earlier campaigns had already swept the empire: 'Veni Vidi Vici' ('I came, I saw, I conquered').

As S. A. Handford says in *Caesar, The Conquest of Gaul:*.

'Even if it was not time for a campaign that season, Caesar thought it would be of great advantage to him merely to visit the island, to see what its inhabitants were like and to make himself acquainted with the lie of the land, the harbours and the landing places. Of all this the Gauls knew next to nothing.'

Caesar withdrew his army from Germany and throughout July of 55BC marched westwards towards the Gallic shore somewhere between what is today Calais and Boulogne. Here, Caesar's men, aboard their Roman galleys, were forced to learn rapidly about the indiosyncracies of these strange waters. The tides were unlike those in the Mediterranean. Storms were more frequent and more severe than they had ever encountered before. With no maritime forecasting available to him, the only invasion strategy Caesar could make was to pick a fine spell before setting off for the island of Britannia. August, he decided, was as good a month as any.

And so, on 25 August 55BC, Julius Caesar landed in Britain. It is likely he came ashore at Walmer, near Deal in Kent. The Britons were there to meet him. The enemy Islanders, with their chariots and horsemen advanced into the sea to challenge the invaders. Caesar's transports and warships grounded in deeper water. The legionaries, uncertain of the depth, hesitated in a shower of javelins and stones. Eventually, Caesar brought his ships and his men firing catapults upon the British flank. Then, as the Romans leaped into the sea, there followed a short, ferocious fight. But the Romans reached the shore and forced the islanders to flee.

Left: *This drawing shows Maiden Castle, in Dorset, around the time of the Roman Conquest. It was arguably England's greatest southern hill fort and an important centre of government for Celtic chiefs. The Romans took it after a heavy battle.*

Above: *A general view of the amphitheatre at Corinium (now known as Cirencester), one of Roman Britain's principal towns.*

Below: *The ruins of the Roman Pharos at Dover Castle as they appear today. The site was strategically important and the fort was among the first built by the Romans in the second century and supported a squadron of the British fleet. It has been added to and embellished down the centuries.*

Caesar and his men were to spend a three-week reconnaissance on the island. It was, on reflection, a singularly unimpressive visit. Caesar hardly moved from his camp at the landing place except to see off another attacking British force. When he eventually set off on his journey home to Gaul, it was without 12 of the vessels and a substantial number of men with which he had set out. He had paid dearly for his inexperience of sea storms.

Caesar was later to admit:

'A number of ships were shattered and the rest, having lost their cables, anchors and the remainder of their tackle, were unusable, which naturally threw the whole army into great consternation/ For they had no other vessels in which they could return, not any materials for repairing the fleet, and since it had been generally understood that they were to return to Gaul for the winter, they had not provided themselves with a stock of grain for wintering in Britain.'

Caesar was well aware his expedition had not been a great success. Nevertheless, he did get safely home, and with a few islanders as hostages. Furthermore he had decided to return to the island the following year – this time for a real invasion.

In 54BC, Caesar was again approaching the Kent coast. His arrival was far more awesome than the last time. For now he had 800 ships and the Islanders stood no chance of holding back his invasion from landing on their shores. But again, the weather was to cause Caesar problems. Raging storms battered a great number of his ships and he had to retrace the 19 kilometres (12 miles) he and

his army had marched inland, back to the shore to haul the vessels ashore. This was no mean feat and took 10 days.

It also provided an excellent opportunity for the Britons. As the War Commentaries of Caesar reports:

'While this work was going on, one legion had been sent out as usual to bring in grain… Since the grain in this area had all been cut except for what was in one place, the enemy guessed where our men would go and lay hidden in the woods during the night. Then when our men, their arms laid aside, were scattered and busy reaping, they suddenly burst out on them, killed a few and threw the rest into confusion before they could form up, swarming around them with cavalry and chariots..'

But then Caesar was on the march again, cutting down all Britons he found sheltering in forests. He crossed the Thames near Brentford. Conquering this strange island looked a simple business, but Caesar did not anticipate the intervention of a mysterious figure called Cassivellaunus.

The Britons had found a leader in this chief Cassivellaunus, a master of war in conditions which were alien to their invaders. Dismissing the rag taggle army of peasants who formed to fight Caesar, Cassivellaunus kept pace with the enemy march by march with his chariots and horsemen. Caesar gave a detailed description of the tactics:

'In chariot-fighting, the Britons begin by driving all over the field hurling javelins, and generally the terror inspired by the horses and the noise of the wheels are sufficient to throw their opponents' ranks into disorder. Then, after making their way between the squadrons of their own cavalry, they jump down from the chariots and engage on foot. In the meantime, their charioteers retire a short distance from the battle and place the chariots in such a position that their masters, if hard pressed by numbers. have an easy means of retreat to their own lines. Thus they combine the mobility of cavalry with the staying power of infantry; and by daily training and practice they attain such proficiency that even on a steep incline they are able to control the horses at full gallop and to check and turn them in a moment. They can run along the chariot pole as quick as lightning.'

Cassivellaunus's other tactic was to cut off Caesar's foraging parties. It was all a noble and brave effort, but Caesar captured his first major stronghold and attempts to destroy his shoreside base failed. The time had come for talking. Cassivellaunus negotiated the surrender of hostages and terms of submission. In turn, Caesar agreed to leave the island. He had finally triumphed — and gladly turned his face for Rome. There he was greeted as a world-conquering hero. In 45BC Emperor Caesar attained absolute power, ushering in Rome's golden age. The following year he was assassinated.

It would take another 100 years until the Emperor Claudius was able to conquer Britain. Until then, the British Islanders had been left in peace, building up trade with Rome and happily accepting Roman traders in their midst. It was, for its time, an ideal situation. But sadly, it was this idyll which once more brought the island to the attention of the greedy empire, as reports of the wealth and possibilities of a stable government increasingly interested those back in Rome. Eventually, they began to tantalise Emperor Claudius who was determined to cast off his reputation as simple and ineffectual.

Above: *The great Roman fort at Richborough, in Kent, from the air and* (**Above Right**) *a close-up view of its earthwork fortifications.*

Right: *Portchester Castle, above Portsmouth Harbour, was one of the forts of the Litus Saxonicum (Saxon Shore) and was built principally to counter sea-borne landings by Germanic pirates. It was occupied for much of the fourth century.*

Far Right: *The remnants of Roman architecture at the town of Venta Icenorum, in Caister-by-Norwich, Norfolk.*

Storming Britain was the ideal way to do it.

In 43AD Claudius's invasion fleet, under Aulus Plautius, landed at Richborough, on the Kent shores. It comprised an army of some 20,000 men — and the islanders were not expecting them. The Romans marched inland, easily winning the first of their skirmishes with the British. Then onwards towards the River Medway, where a fierce two-day battle was fought. Togodumnus, a British resistance leader, died in the fighting. His brother, Caractacus fled north-westwards with the surviving troops, believing that the Romans would try to cross the river by bridge. But Roman auxiliary troops moved upstream to ford the river and launch a pre-emptive strike, shooting down the horses of the feared British charioteers. Legionaries under Flavius Vespasianus (the future emperor Vespasian) and his brother Sabinus then crossed the river despite strong resistance, and an offensive led by Hosidius Geta the next morning finally put the Britons to flight.

By the summer of 43AD, the south-east of Britain and the Isle of Wight had fallen to the Romans. To mark his victories, Emperor Claudius presided at an awesome surrender ceremony at Colchester, the capital of the defeated Trinovantes tribe. There was a grand parade which included the emperor's personal bodyguard — and elephants. No one dared mention that this was the emperor's first real visit to the battle-torn island. Until now, while the fighting raged he had awaited news of his invasion from the safety of France. Only after Vespasian's victory did Claudius cross the Channel, bringing his elephants and reinforcements with him.

But the invaders were having trouble taking command of other areas. The westerly Atrebates tribe and the fierce Durotriges tribe of Dorset stood their ground. Further west still, the Dumnonii tribes of Devon and Cornwall remained outside Roman control. But the 2nd legion of Romans under Vespasian slowly advanced across the island, cutting down their British foes.

The invaders had become particularly skilled at attacking the islanders' earthwork hill fortresses. First an artillery barrage showered the defenders with a lethal iron rain forcing them off the ramparts. A direct infantry assault would follow as the Britons scrabbled around to find cover. Forts such as Badbury Rings and Maiden Castle soon fell. By the middle of 44AD, the Roman invasion of Britain was complete.

The brave Caractacus was still on the run, however, taking refuge in swamps and forests. He was to muster tribes and continue the resistance against the Romans for six long years. He was finally betrayed by his compatriot, Queen Cartimandua of the northerly Brigantes, who handed him over to the Romans. What happened next shows remarkable presence of mind by Caractacus. Paraded through Rome, watched by thousands to whom his name had become legend, he refused to bow his head or show fear. Instead, he boldly approached where the Emperor was sitting and made this speech:

'If to my high birth and distinguished rank I had added the virtues of moderation Rome had beheld me rather as a friend than a captive, you would not have rejected an alliance with a prince descended from illustrious ancestors and governing many nations. The reverse of my fortune to you is glorious and to me humiliating. I had arms and men and horses. I possessed extraordinary riches and can it be any wonder that I was unwilling to lose them? Because Rome aspires to universal dominion must men therefore implicitly resign themselves to subjection? I opposed for a long time

the progress of your arms and had I acted otherwise, would either you have had the glory of conquest or I of a brave resistance? I am now in your power. If you are determined to take revenge, my fate will soon be forgotten and you will derive no honour from the transaction. Preserve my life and I shall remain to the latest ages a monument of your clemency.'

Claudius granted Caractacus his liberty, saying he was free to live with his family in Rome. Meanwhile back in Britain, Queen Cartimandua was well rewarded for her loyalty to Rome and betrayal of Caractacus: in the form of Roman handouts and luxury goods.

Claudius died in 54AD, possibly from eating poisoned mushrooms. He was succeeded by Nero, his 17-year-old adopted son. Nero did not find peace easy to maintain in those early days of his furthest-flung province.

In 60AD the southern British Iceni tribe rose up in rebellion after the humliation of seeing their leader Boudicca (or Boadicea, as she was later known) flogged and her daughters raped. The Iceni were backed by the Trinovantes, much of whose land had been confiscated to support the colony of Roman veterans at Colchester. The major Roman settlements, Camulodunum, Londinium and Verulamium (Colchester, London and St Albans) were stormed, and their inhabitants slaughtered with great cruelty. The governor, Suetonius Paulinus, was campaigning in North Wales when the rebellion broke out, met the rebel forces somewhere in the Midlands and crushed them. Boudicca herself died, probably by committing suicide, and the Iceni and their allies were then 'pacified' with typical Roman brutality.

After relative calm was restored in Britain, the conquerors were forced to turn their attention homewards. The Roman civil war, which began with Nero's suicide in 68AD, was the first of a series of internal conflicts that periodically weakened the Roman military effort and presence in Britain. Nevertheless, the pace of advance resumed in 71AD with the subjugation of the Brigantes of northern England (71-74), the subjugation of most of Wales (73-6) and, during the governorship of Cnaeus Julius Agricola (77-83), the completion of the conquests of Wales and northern England.

The Romans also attempted the conquest of Scotland but their hold there was always tenuous — and these northern reaches finally proved to be the furthest outpost of their empire. Agricola, having marched into southern Scotland with the Ninth Legion In 81AD, advanced to a front-line position betwixt the estuaries of the Rivers Clyde and Forth. He built a chain of forts across the land, sustained by the Roman fleet, and in 83AD Agricola vanquished the local Caledonians in the battle of Mons Graupius, believed to be the Hill of Moncrieffe.

We know of these events from the writings of the Roman historian Tacitus, who happened to be Agricola's son-in-law. Tacitus wrote proudly of his relation's victories, principally against the Caledonian chieftain Calgacus, but criticised subsequent Roman strategy. For in 84AD, only months after Agricola had subdued the Lowland Scots, the general received sudden orders from Rome to withdraw. As Tacitus wrote: 'Perdomita Britannia et statim omissa' (Britain is conquered then is at once thrown away).

Imperial strategy became defensive rather than offensive. The Emperor Hadrian himself visited Britain in 121AD and ordered the building of new defences along a line back into England far south of Agricola's earlier frontier. The famous Hadrian's Wall, between

Above: *The quality and structure of Roman roads was such that many can still be found today across England. Here a typically straight example stretches out for more than a mile across Wheeldale high up in the North Yorkshire Moors, not far from Goathland.*

Above Right: *A superb example of intricate geometric patterning on a Roman mosaic as it appears on a pavement in the old town of Isurium Brigantum, now Aldborough in the vale of York.*

Right: *A Roman coin bearing the head of the Emperor Trajan (98-117AD). Finds such as this one, which turned up during excavations at the Stanwick Iron Age site, are relatively common.*

the estuaries of the Solway and the Tyne, was to be a deterrent to the raiding parties of the factionalised northern tribes, particularly the Picts. This most impressive of structures, eventually comprising a stone wall 113 kilometres (70 miles) long with supporting forts known as 'housesteads', still stands today for most of its length.

Less than 20 years later, however, the new Emperor Antoninus Pius ordered the restoration of Roman rule over the defiant northerners. Within months of succeeding Hadrian in 138AD, the tough new emperor decided to abandon Hadrian's Wall, which was still being modified, and push the frontier back to Agricola's earlier positions, some 120 kilometres (75 miles) further north. The then governor of Britain, Lollius Urbisuc, was given the task of constructing the Antonine Wall during the years following 142AD. It ran for about 60 kilometres (37 miles) across the narrow waist of Scotland formed by the Rivers Forth and Clyde.

Roman armies were now defending an empire which extended from the Clyde to the Euphrates. Who were these soldiers charged with the task of defending the province of Britain, first from behind Hadrian's Wall and then the Antonine Wall? At the start, most of them would be highly trained legionaries; not necessarily Romans but possibly mercenaries and local recruits. Most of the summer they would have spent north of the walls on patrol, chasing off raiders and supervising the local tribes. Workers for the maintenance of the walls would have been mainly local in origin. For like the Britons in the south, the Pictish-Scottish inhabitants of the north were now beginning to learn the long, slow lesson of living as neighbours with the Romans. For a while, uneasy peace reigned in the north of Britain.

It was only when the Romans tried to push their boundaries still further northwards that the remaining warlike tribes retaliated. In 208AD the Emperor Severus, having vanquished half of the near-East, ordered the conquest of all Scotland. The Caledonian defenders had learned their military lessons, however, and rather than confronting the disciplined Roman ranks in pitched battle, fought guerrilla warfare through the Grampian mountains and forests. Severus, who had been personally supervising the invasion, returned to his northern British headquarters at Eboracum (York) and died. Encouraged, the Caledonian tribes again went on the offensive. The Romans abandoned the Antonine Wall and fell back to the older Hadrian's Wall, which for the next 100 years remained the northern frontier of Rome. The far north of Britain was again cast into the mists of little-recorded history.

The Romans were not to persist in their attempts to unite all Britain militarily. Plans for the total subjugation of Ireland were shelved in part due to the competing demands of the vulnerable Danube frontier, which also meant a reduction in the considerable military effort devoted to Britain, just as earlier Nero had withdrawn troops in preparation for campaigning on the Asian frontier of the empire.

Despite the costly military presence that typified all frontier provinces, Roman territorial ambition gradually gave way to peaceful co-existence. It was peace not war which ensured the direct Roman impact on England for a full half-millennium — about 330 years of which (from 78-409AD) the whole of England and Wales was ruled by imperial Rome.

This period is the real starting point of the fully recorded history of England, not only because of its political unity, but also simply because Roman remains provide us with information about what life was like. Christianity, introduced in the late second cen-

tury and organised into dioceses by the early fourth century, also meant the spread of literacy and the better recording of events.

From the writings left to us by chroniclers, generals and churchmen, it is abundantly clear that the four centuries of Roman rule brought a prolific growth in culture and communications. This intensification of all the progress which had taken place in the previous 1,500 years was tempered by economic and political changes — and even an early sense of 'ecological' responsibility as the new rulers curbed the over-exploitation of the land itself.

Roman Britain displayed the characteristics of other imperial provinces. The settlement of people from elsewhere in the empire, many of them ex-soldiers, was matched by the Romanization of the British elite. The word civilisation is from the Latin 'civis' (a city), and the Romans instituted what would now be termed a 'construction boom'. Towns appeared where there had previously only been hill forts. By the mid-second century, London, the lowest bridging point on the Thames, had become the capital and the major port of Roman Britain. York, Chester and Caerleon were the permanent bases of three legions, while Colchester, Lincoln and Gloucester were 'coloniae': towns founded for veterans. Provincial capitals included Canterbury, Chichester, Winchester, Dorchester, Exeter, Cirencester, St Albans, Leicester and Carmarthen.

Gridded street plans developed in these towns. The streets were bordered by shops and houses, centring on communal buildings, such as baths, temples, theatres and the forum. Roman engineers diverted rivers to aid planning, as in Winchester, Chichester and Cirencester. 600 or more country villas were built (the Latin word 'villa' simply means a farm), all constructed in a Roman style and heated from under the floor by a hypocaust system. These buildings, floored with mosaics, must have appeared magnificent households, extolling the obvious virtues of Roman culture to the conquered Britons who still lived in timber and mud huts.

9,600 kilometres (6,000 miles) of roads linked the Roman towns, villas and garrisons. Many of these roads are still used today — the A5, for example, follows the route of old Watling Street. Roads, remarkably straight as can be seen from any modern map, were built to a high standard, with stone foundations and gravel surfaces. They constituted a planned network, testimony to the impact of a powerful governmental structure that also organised a large-scale drainage scheme in East Anglia. Finally, and of course most importantly, there was an effective taxation system, partly to fund and supply the standing army.

As goods and money were regularly moved across greater distances, including to and from the Continent, inter-regional contact increased and new fashions and designs were disseminated, as in the pottery industry. The greater quantity of archaeological material surviving from the Roman period suggests a society producing and trading far more goods than its Iron Age predecessors.

Roman religious cults spread, though assimilation with native Celtic beliefs was important. When Christianity became the state religion further cultural links between England and the Continent were forged. The druids, whom the Romans had stamped out, and the cults of the Olympian gods, which they had originally introduced themselves, lacked doctrinal regulation and any diocesan structure. Pagan practices continued, however, and outside the lowland towns and centres of imperial authority and culture, Britain was not as thoroughly Romanised as other provinces of the empire, such as Gaul.

However, the introduction of more sophisticated farming

implements — scythes, for instance, were unknown before the Romans — and the peaceful centuries which followed the settlement of England led to an unprecedented prosperity, with a consequent further growth in the population of the British Isles of about four million.

But Roman Britain suffered from one recurring flaw: the greed for power among the imperial elite. The province was weakened by the inability of the Roman empire to devise a consistently accepted system of imperial successions, and by the willingness of military units to support their commanders in bids for power. In 296 Britain had to be invaded in order to defeat a rebel Roman leader. These upheavals interacted cumulatively with the burden of defending Roman Britain from outside challenges, including Picts from Scotland, Scots from Ireland and Saxons from northern Germany and southern Scandinavia. Their attacks became serious in the 350s, while a successful invasion in 367 led to widespread devastation. Order was restored by Theodosius 368-69. The construction of town defences from the third century indicated an increasingly 'siege mentality'.

Civil war in the empire and barbarian invasions led to new problems in the 400s. In 406 Gaul was invaded by a vast number of barbarians. Britain, threatened with being cut off from the rest of the empire, created its own emperor who took a significant part of the island's military forces to counter the barbarian threat. They did not return. In 410 the Britons, disillusioned with the rebel Constantine IIIs activities, expelled his administrators and appealed to the true Emperor, Honorius, for the restoration of legitimate rule. He, hard pressed in Italy by Alaric, the Visigoth leader who captured Rome that year, could do no more than tell them to look to their own defence.

This was the end of the Roman empire in Britain. The history of England was about to take another, violent turn.

Above: *More coins recovered from the Stanwick site.*

Below: *Looking west towards an old Roman wall at St Albans in Hertfordshire. Roman architecture must have been a revelation to any Celtic tribe which had direct contact with the invaders.*

Above Left: *Roman building sites were organised, highly efficient places – and there was never a shortage of cheap labour. This drawing shows a gang constructing the city walls at Silchester, near Reading.*

Below Left: *Looking down on Silchester, one of England's most impressive Roman cities, in its heyday.*

Above: *A closer look within the city walls at Silchester which the Romans called Calleva Atrebatum. The great square building would have served both as a barracks and the centre of local government.*

Right: *The view as it is today at Corbridge, on Hadrian's Wall. The Romans never conquered Scotland and the wall, begun in 122AD, was designed as a first defence against marauding bands of Scottish tribes heading south.*

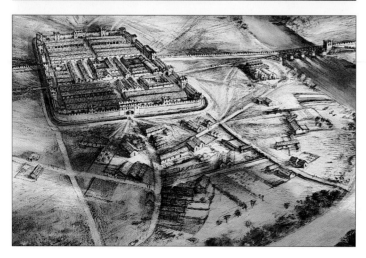

Above: *Hardknott Roman Fort on the Wrynose Pass, Cumbria.*

Left: *Walltown Crags, Hadrian's Wall, as it would have been seen by its Roman defenders. For many years it was thought the wall had suffered two great destruction's by northern tribes – in 197AD and 296. Many archaeologists now believe this scenario is flawed.*

Below Left: *The impressive Chesters Fort, on Hadrian's Wall, was a vital strategic garrison on the Roman empire's north-west frontier. To the soldiers who served there however, the isolation and the long, freezing winters must have made it a posting to dread.*

Opposite: *Brunton Turret as it probably looked shortly after construction in the 2nd century AD. These signalling turrets were interspersed with fortlets every mile, along with 16 larger garrisons spread along the 120km (75 mile) stretch of the wall.*

Overleaf: *Chesters Fort.*

THE LEGEND OF CAMELOT

By the end of the fourth century, the last isolated Roman outposts along the Roman empire's northern boundaries were being abandoned. Troubles closer to home were presaging the collapse of the mightiest empire the world had ever known. One by one, the legions were recalled from Britain to defend their Mediterranean trade routes. By 430AD the whole of Britain had been abandoned.

The fifth century is a particularly obscure period, but it is clear that, despite the mythology that has built up around these Dark Ages, a measure of social continuity existed. Rather than being a period simply of conquest and resistance, the collapse of one regime and the rise of another, the situation was far more complex. Romanised town and villa life, and the practice of Christianity, did not cease abruptly, and archaeological evidence of violent destruction is limited. Nevertheless, as elsewhere in western Europe, 'barbarian' mercenaries were hired and came to demand power for themselves. Alongside continuity in, for example, Kent, many other regions of Britain fell into the pre-Roman pattern of warring tribes.

In the north, the departure of the legions encouraged the ever bolder Caledonian tribes to push further and further south. But they soon encountered a mass movement of humanity that was imploding upon the British Isles in the vacuum left by the departing Romans. Teutonic invaders, the Jutes, the Angles and the Saxons, swarmed across the North Sea to plunder the countryside. They drove the native Britons westwards and northwards, back into the West Country, the Welsh borders and southern Scotland. The influx of these Germanic invaders in the fifth century was modest in terms of numbers, but their effect on the previously well-ordered, Romanised British society was cataclysmic.

The defenders of Britain could no longer call for assistance from the Continent to beat off the invaders, as they had in the fourth century. Moreover, being divided into warring kingdoms, their assailants were able to marshal their forces in ever-growing bases in lowland England. The Celtic natives, forced ever westwards, were desperately in need of a unifying leader to rally around.

Romano-British resistance was not uniformly unsuccessful, however, and in about 500 it achieved a major victory — supposedly at Mons Badonicus and under a warrior leader of the period called Artorius. One of the most enduring, inspiring and romantic legends in history was born...

The man was called 'The Once And Future King' — and certainly his heroic exploits survived the centuries to inspire and to intrigue. Legend has it that King Arthur battled to save his Celtic Britons from the invading Saxon armies. In a barbarous age, he ruled his people with benevolence and justice for all. His Knights of the Round Table came to epitomise everything that is chivalrous in human endeavour. His capital, Camelot, has become a byword for all that is gentle, noble, virtuous, righteous and learned.

So who was King Arthur? Did he really, as the ancient tales tell us, have a wizard called Merlin, a queen named Guinevere, a sword Excalibur, a round table, an island of Avalon and a fabulous castle called Camelot? Indeed, did this monarch and his noblest of champions truly exist — or is Arthur simply the most enduring and fascinating myth of English folklore?

The earliest reference to such a king is in the seventh-century epic Welsh poem Gododdin, which speaks of a 'mighty warrior' in the continuing battles against the Saxons. There is little historical doubt that about 200 years before the poem was written a valiant leader did indeed live in the West of England and Welsh Borders around the year 518AD. It is likely that the man now known as King Arthur was a Romanised military leader who united the battle-weary peasants before turning the tide of war against the Anglo-Saxons.

Some historians believe he may even have been the military mastermind behind a little-known British general, Ambrosius Aurelianus, whose armies when pushed back to the Welsh borders by the advancing Saxons, stood and fought at the Battle of Mount Badon in 518. Largely thanks to the tactical genius of one of his chieftains, known only as Arthur, the English army defeated the occupiers so convincingly that peace was restored in the region for half a century.

Early Welsh scribes called Arthur 'a king of wonders and marvels' and the Arthurian legend took on a life of its own. In 1135 Geoffrey of Monmouth described Arthur in his Historia as the conqueror of western Europe. That is obviously far from the truth; Arthur's reign was over only a region of old England. In the 12th century another work, Roman De Bru, elaborated on Arthur's prowess and imbued him with the qualities of chivalry and piety that have remained interlocked with his legend ever since.

Knights were added to Arthur's court by the French poet Chrestien de Troyes. In his 13th century romance Perceval, these valiant knights embark on a quest for the Holy Grail, the chalice from which Christ drank at the Last Supper. Sir Gawain And The Green Knight, published around 1370, was the next major work to reinforce the legend. Then came Morte d'Arthur by Sir Thomas Mallory, the most important and certainly the most detailed mediaeval account of the Arthurian legend.

It is strange how the story of Camelot grew to reflect the aspirations of the peasantry of Britain, with its strange mixture of Christian beliefs and pagan wizardry. But how can one sift the fact from the fable — for fact there certainly is in the legend of this English warlord?

Right: *The Roman city of Viroconium (Wroxeter), Shropshire. Folklorists have speculated that this was the site of Camelot, from where Arthur, a Romanised Briton, unified the native Celtic peasantry against Anglo-Saxon invaders.*

Supposedly, Arthur was the illegitimate son of Uther Pendragon, King of Britain, and his mistress Igraine. Upon Uther's death, Arthur inherited his throne simply by publicly declaring it was rightfully his. It was at this time, too, that Arthur pulled the legendary sword Excalibur from a block of stone. Engraved on the stone were the words: 'Whosoever pulls this sword from the stone and anvil is the rightful king of England.' Folklore has it that no one claiming the throne had achieved this before. Thus Arthur, who until this point had been brought up in secret and whose existence was not even known to most, became the rightful heir. Merlin, the court wizard who was to become Arthur's mentor, bowed down before him and proclaimed him king.

However, Arthur's success was not immediate. Contrary to what legend would have us believe, there were many years of fierce fighting before Arthur's right to the kingdom was accepted. Not everyone loved and revered him but he protected himself and his realm by instituting the glorious regime of his famous Round Table Knights. And he married a beautiful bride, Guinevere (actually his second wife).

Arthur's principal enemies included his own treacherous sister, Morgan la Fay, and his nephew, Mordred. Morgan was a witch who plotted against her brother and once, while Arthur was away in battle, seized the throne. Arthur eventually killed Mordred, but not before he was fatally wounded himself. His body was buried on the holy isle of Avalon, where it was believed a miracle would one day take place and restored him to life. That burial place is still undisturbed.

So much for the legend. What of the facts that support the existence of such a man and his court? The two keys are the location of 'Camelot' and 'Avalon'. We know that a war leader who fitted the Arthurian image did indeed live in England's West Country and Welsh Borders around the year 518AD. But the legends that embellished his brief history might have remained no more than folklore but for research into the chronicles of Glastonbury Abbey in Somerset.

Writing in about 1120, William Malmesbury had described Arthur's grave as having been discovered in the oldest part of the cemetery of the Abbey's Lady Chapel. The grave was marked by a cross inscribed (in Latin) with the words: 'Here lies the famous King Arthur with Guinevere, his second wife, buried in the Island of Avalon.'

This story conformed with the records of the Abbey. Some of the more important graves had been excavated in the tenth century as the level of the cemetery was raised. According to a Bishop Dunstan, the new surface level was protected by a wall. If the monks had gone to this trouble, it would have been logical to erect a fresh stone over the grave of Arthur and Guinevere. The abbey records also contain a report that in 1190 Abbot Henry of Sully exhumed the royal coffin from a pit about 5 metres (16 feet) deep and removed it to the Abbey's treasury.

Glastonbury received two other royal visitors in 1275 — this time live ones. King Edward I and his Queen Eleanor made a pilgrimage to consecrate the abbey's high altar. On this auspicious occasion, the abbot broke open the treasury's ancient coffin to reveal two caskets, each decorated with coats of arms. In one was the skeleton of a tall man, in the other was that of a slightly-built woman. They were rewrapped in shrouds and presumably returned to the vaults or reburied.

In 1960 archaeologists excavated the area within Glastonbury Abbey where Arthur's grave might have been. They discovered that a deep pit had once been dug out and refilled with the indent of a headstone above it. But of the bones of King Arthur and his queen there was unfortunately no sign.

But why should the Somerset town of Glastonbury, which is well inland, ever have been called the Isle of Avalon? In Arthurian times, the place was an isolated area of high ground surrounded by marshland, effectively turning it into an island. In Welsh, it is known as Ynys Avallon, meaning the Island of Apples.

If Glastonbury was Avalon, where was Camelot? The conflict at which Arthur was reputedly killed was known as the Battle of Camlann and is believed to have taken place near Cadbury, Somerset, site of an ancient castle. Thousands of man-hours have gone into excavations there but archaeologists still have not found proof of the existence of Camelot, its knights or the most romantic king in British history.

The reason, according to fresh evidence unearthed in 1995, is that Camelot may be nowhere near Cadbury — nor even the West Country. The site of the mythical castle, it is claimed by some, may well be a marshy field about 13 kilometres (8 miles) outside Shrewsbury, Shropshire. It is possible that Arthur was in fact a king of Powys, a powerful dynasty that ruled much of Britain's western boundaries after the Romans departed. Their power base was the old city of Veraconium, now mere ruins outside the town of Wroxeter, and their burial place was known as the 'chapels of Bassa', believed to be the small village of Baschurch, outside Shrewsbury. Archaeologists have established that the site was once a Dark Ages fort surrounded by water — remarkably similar to the mythical Camelot.

Right: *Few legends have captured the imagination of English storytellers as strongly as Camelot. Standing stones and burial chambers from an earlier age were often linked to his adventures, as with Arthur's Stone at Dorstone, near Hereford.*

Below: *Glastonbury Tor, in Somerset, was a medieval settlement thought by some to be the burial place of King Arthur.*

Below Left: *The 1193 exhumation of bodies, said to be those of Arthur and Guinevere, at Glastonbury Abbey.*

TINTAGEL CASTLE

Tintagel Castle situated high up on the Cornish cliffs remains one of the most spectacular and romantic spots in all England, destined to remain a place of mystery and romance long associated with the Arthurian legend.

The story goes that King Arthur lived in a castle here, and Merlin the magician lived in a cave on the beach. Is it the place the Romans called Durocornovium? Was it a Celtic Christian monastery? was it the stronghold of the kings of Cornwall in the Dark Ages? Questions like these add to the magic and mystery of Tintagel, balanced perilously between a rocky promontory and the mainland.

What is clear is that the present castle was laid out in the13th century by Richard, Earl of Cornwall, younger brother of Henry II, and that by Tudor times it had fallen into the ruins seen now. The keep on the mainland is thought to date from 1236-72, and the remains of the chapel on the summit of the promontory are thought to be 13th century as well.

But the site was obviously occupied before this. It was probably the stronghold of the Earls of Cornwall from about 1150. The numerous ruined buildings dotted around the promontory probably date from the same period. Recent excavations have uncovered traces of a Celtic monastery occupied from around 500 to 850. There may even have been a Roman signal station here to warn ships, by smoke signals, that an invasion was imminent.

Below: *The inner ward and great hall at Tintagel Castle, on Cornwall's rugged Atlantic coast. It is one of the most famous and mysterious sites of Dark Age England and is said to have been Arthur's birthplace. The ruins have yielded evidence of both a medieval castle and a monastery but there is no other known castle which bears direct comparison.*

Right: *On a stormy day the mouth of Merlin's Cave, below Tintagel, exudes a magical atmosphere.*

THE DARK AGES

According to The Anglo-Saxon Chronicle, the kingdom of Kent was founded in the 450s by Jutes under the possibly mythical Hengist and Horsa. Sources for this invasion period are scant and often unreliable. Indeed, The Anglo-Saxon Chronicle was not written until much later, probably in King Alfred's reign, and the Germanic invaders themselves were illiterate. However, archaeological evidence does prove there was a strong Germanic invasion of Angles, Saxons and Jutes from northern Germany and Denmark, with the latter establishing themselves in Kent, the Isle of Wight and parts of Hampshire. The more dominant Saxons founded the kingdom of Wessex in the upper Thames Valley, around Dorchester-on-Thames, and expanded its power into Hampshire. And the Angles, although not the strongest presence in the conquered lands, nevertheless were to give their name to the nation we now call England.

Britain was taking on a new shape, created from conquest and tribal differences.

The sixth century saw yet more cultural and community changes, with certain of the more powerful tribes increasing their domains. The Wessex Saxons spread west and north, while the Angles established kingdoms in the Midlands (Mercia), Yorkshire (Deira), north of the Tees (Bernicia) and East Anglia. Bernicia was probably established at or near Bamburgh in the mid sixth century and Deira, to the north of the Humber, in the late fifth century.

This spread of power by the new settlers continued for over three centuries. Bernicia expanded greatly under Aethelfrith (593-616), reaching as far as Lothian, and also probably pushed back the frontier of North Wales, while Deira gained the vales of York and Pickering. The British kingdoms of Elmet, centred on Leeds, and Rheged, around the Solway estuary, were absorbed by Northumbria (created from Bernicia and Deira) in the late sixth and seventh centuries, although Strathclyde survived. Elsewhere, the spread of these new kingdoms did not go so smoothly. The Saxon occupation of Dorset did not happen until the late sixth or seventh centuries, Cornwall was only conquered by Wessex in 838 and the kingdoms in Wales were never conquered.

In those areas that were conquered, the 'Romano-Britons' largely fled or survived as slaves and peasants. There was, however, a significant drop in the population — partly due to devastating outbreaks of plague. By now, the original British language and culture were largely lost in England.

The former Roman Empire within the country had fallen; but Anglo-Saxon civilisation, such as it was, still inevitably owed much to its predecessors. Farming techniques remained unaltered, with the Anglo-Saxons commandeering land that had already been worked. But the new custodians of England's rich soil did not enjoy wealthy, trouble-free times. With plague and violence raging, people existed on the bare minimum. Evidence of this comes from the excavation of few coins from the period and even fewer 'luxury' possessions. Only a couple of areas have yielded rich and ornate goods — many from the continent and Byzantium — to suggest some successful economic trade. Relics found in cemeteries in Kent and some parts of East Anglia indicate that, while Britain's inland population found life a struggle, coastal dwellers realised the importance and benefits of commercial links with the continent.

The numerous small kingdoms of the sixth century took a long time to merge and form friendly, larger communities. And such a state did not come about without fierce rivalry and wars. Penda of Mercia (c632-654), for instance, was said to have had an army which included forces contributed by 30 subordinate leaders, many of whom would once have been the independent rulers of small territories. The West Midland kingdoms of the Hwicce and the Magonsaetan were absorbed by Mercia which, after the death of King Anna (654), dominated the formerly independent East Anglia. Overkings, or rulers who enjoyed leadership over other kings, such as Aethelbert of Kent in the 590s, found their successes short-term.

For much of the seventh century, most of the power belonged to the rulers of Northumbria. Oswald (634-41), Oswin (641-70) and Egfrith (670-85) ruled the lands between the Humber and the Forth on the eastern side of Britain, and between the Mersey and the Ayr on the west, and were at times treated as overlords by the rulers of Mercia, Wessex, Strathclyde and the Pict and Scottish territories. This hegemony finally ended following defeats at the hands of Mercia in 678 and the Picts in 685, after which Northumbria lost its position as an almighty Anglo-Saxon kingdom. That accolade was now taken by Mercia, while Wessex became more dominant in southern England, conquering the Isle of Wight in 685.

Though records of this period of English history are scant, it seems that settlement in the middle Saxon period — 650 to 850 — were widespread, if scattered. The preferred dwellings were houses and farmsteads which were gathered together within small hamlets. Poorer peasants lived in villages with large numbers of huts with sunken floors. A surviving example of this is at Mucking in Essex. Furthermore it is to the Anglo-Saxons that we owe many of today's place names, with name endings such as 'ham', 'ton' and 'worth'.

A small number of major ports (Ipswich, London, Southampton and York) developed spectacularly in the eighth century and by the 10th century a more extensive urban network was in place. And at least two royal palaces were built in Britain around this time — at Yeavering in Northumberland and at Cheddar in Somerset (which was a rural palace for the kings of Wessex).

Right: *A cross to the memory of St Augustine, a religious philosopher and a major influence on England's first 'national' king, Alfred.*

But what of religious beliefs during this period which came to be known as the Dark Ages? In 597, a monk called Augustine, dispatched by Pope Gregory the Great, led a mission to Canterbury, the capital of Aethelbert's Kent. Augustine had some success at converting the people of the south-east to Christianity — but it was the church of Ireland that was the base for the conversion first of Scotland and then, via Northumbria, of most of England. There was a pagan reaction in Northumbria in 632 but the Christian King Oswald won control there in 634 and, thanks to his influence, Cynegils of Wessex was baptised in 635. Peada, heir to the vigorous pagan Penda of Mercia, followed in 653, although paganism was difficult to eradicate. Signs of pagan burials throughout the Midlands, Essex, Kent and East Anglia have been useful historical indications of Saxon settlements.

There was also tension between the Northumbrian church and the authority of Rome. But, as a result of the support of King Oswy of Northumbria at the Synod of Whitby in 664, Roman customs, such as the date of Easter, prevailed.

Christianity meant stronger links with the Continent. St Wilfrid (634-709), the Abbot of Ripon, studied in Rome, ministered in Lyon, and was consecrated bishop at Compiègne. Bishoprics were created and diocesan boundaries reorganised. A strong monastic tradition — as, for instance, at Jarrow, Monkwearmouth and Lindisfarne — influenced the nature of kingship, since many monasteries were founded by rulers and nobles of the period. From the late seventh century, monastic churches were constructed at important centres, though most local parish churches were not founded until the 10th and 11th centuries.

Christianity meant the beginnings of written law — not least to protect churchmen and their property – and the use of such documents to prove ownership of land. That is not to say that the pen was thought mightier than the sword; military and political strength still determined which kingdoms were to prevail. Skirmishes saw the rise of Offa of Mercia (757-96), who boasted a disciplined society and impressive resources and who controlled such formerly independent kingdoms as Essex, Lindsey, East Anglia, Kent and Sussex. Offa is most often linked with the earth dyke named after him, built to prevent the Welsh from raiding his wealthy kingdom. The combined length of Offa's Dyke (stretches of which still survive today) and the related Wat's Dyke was 240 kilometres (149 miles) — longer than the Antonine and Hadrian's walls — and the building of it must have entailed considerable organisation. It was a testimony to the administrative strength of Mercian England.

Mercia was weakened in the 820s by the effort involved in the occupation of North Wales and by dynastic feuds. Meanwhile further south in 825, after defeating the Mercians at Wroughton, Egbert of Wessex conquered Kent, Essex, Surrey and Sussex. Mercia eventually fell to Egbert in 829 and Cornwall in 838. In 829, Northumbria also acknowledged his overlordship. This acceptance did not last for long however, and Mercia was soon independent again.

Thus, feuds within and between royal families and between tribes ensured that society of Anglo-Saxon England remained violent and unpredictable. As proclaimed in the epic poem Beowulf, it was believed glory could only be achieved through warfare.

Opposite: *An artist's impression of the Sutton Hoo ship burial by Peter Dunn.*

THE VIKING
SCOURGE

Meanwhile, the Vikings had arrived — and for the Saxons who farmed Britain it was the dawn of a terrifying new age. The year was 793 and their prosperous world was about to be turned on its head. Few, if any, had even considered that their wealth would be a target for plunderers from across the sea. Certainly none could have imagined the ruthless, bloodthirsty warriors who would soon be pouring onto their shores.

As for the tall, fair-haired invaders from the Scandinavia, they must have been astounded at the lack of resistance they met. Very often their sleek longboats would come racing towards a beach to be confronted by locals standing around gaping in disbelief. It was never much of a fight. The well-armed, powerful Vikings would slaughter all who crossed their path before stripping nearby villages of valuables or livestock and putting back to sea. Even if the Saxons had a mind to organise defences, it would have been an impossible task; there was no telling when or where the enemy would strike next and the remote coastal settlements of northern and eastern England had no hope of summoning reinforcements in time. It meant rich easy pickings for the raiders, and a typical ship carrying 30 or so men was usually more than sufficient to see off the native opposition.

So who were the Vikings — or Northmen as they were first called — and what drove them to make war? The Vikings originated from the lands that are now Norway, Sweden and Denmark.

The Norwegian people tended to build their settlements around fjords, sheer-sided sunken valleys penetrating far inland and well-protected from the worst of the weather. Some historians believe the name Viking may actually stem from the old Icelandic word 'vic' which describes an sea inlet or cove. The Norwegians were excellent seamen but their agricultural land was limited by the country's topography.

Sweden was easier to cultivate because the land was generally lower and flatter but the winters were much colder and longer than those in Norway. The farmers had only a short growing season and the frozen rivers made travel and trade difficult.

Denmark's problem was the quality of crops. Although the country was low and flat and the climate reasonably mild, much of the land was covered by thin, unproductive soil. Denmark had to rely on its position at the centre of trading routes across the Baltic Sea and the Atlantic for its prosperity.

Shortage of good farmland was certainly one reason why young Vikings took to their ships in search of a better life. Any rise in the Scandinavian population quickly led to a food crisis. This didn't matter much to the wealthier chieftains or 'jarls' who owned most of the land, but it badly affected the middle classes, known as 'karls', who tended to be farmers, tradesmen or sailors. Lowest of the low were the 'thralls', or slaves, they had the worst-paid and dirtiest jobs and were happy to take on a hazardous sea adventure if it meant

Above: *An example of a stone grave marker, in Viking style, dating from the late 9th century AD. The figures represent an attack on either a Scottish or Scandinavian settlement.*

Opposite: *The Brough of Birsay from where Viking lords ruled a substantial empire and set out for the rich pickings of coastal England.*

even the slightest chance of improving their lot.

To make matters worse the size of farms tended to grow smaller. A farmer would divide his land among his sons when he grew too old or sick to continue himself, and these smaller farms were less efficient. No surprise that a majority even of the landed classes decided it was easier to take than to grow...

The limited amount of land available for cultivation in Scandinavia and the vulnerability of nearby prosperous and fertile lands overseas led to an explosion of activity from the late eighth to the late eleventh centuries. The most dramatic results were the establishment of Swedish power in Russia and Norwegian settlements in Iceland, Greenland and possibly Newfoundland (Vinland). In western Europe, the Danes campaigned extensively in northern France, establishing themselves in Normandy. The British Isles, close to Scandinavia and with a long coastline prone to marine raids and invasion, were extensively attacked. The Norwegians overran the Orkney and Shetland islands, the far north of Scotland and much of its west coast, as well as coastal regions of Ireland.

The Viking raiders inspired such terror that for more than 300

years all of Europe lived in fear of their coming. The appearance of these warriors must have been awesome: their main weapons of attack were the two-edged iron sword, heavy battleaxe, a hefty 'stabbing' spear and a lighter 'throwing' spear. They would also use bows and arrows. In defence, a warrior relied upon his large, round shield, a helmet and a mail shirt. One Arab traveller, who had seen them fight at close quarters, wrote:

'The Vikings are a mighty nation, with huge bodies and great courage. They do not know the meaning of the word defeat — they never turn their backs on their enemies but slay or are slain. It is customary for each warrior to carry with him some craftsmen's tools, such as axe, saw, hammer and so on, while he is wearing his armour. He fights on foot with spear and shield. He wears a sword and dagger and has a throwing spear slung across his back.'

The Vikings were not very well disciplined fighters — war for them was very much a 'death or glory' affair. They had little time for tactics if it meant a delay in engaging the enemy, whom they preferred to catch unawares with a ferocious wave of warriors. They even had 'shock troops', the so called 'Beserkers', who according to the Ynglinga Saga 'were frenzied like mad dogs and wolves, biting their shields in their fury. They were as strong as bears or wild boars and struck men down right and left. Neither fire nor steel could stop them.'

England had been free from continental invasion for two centuries but in 789 the Danish ships were first recorded, and in 793-94 the pagan Danes brutally sacked the great Northumbrian monasteries of Lindisfarne and Jarrow. Viking pressure increased in the 830s and 840s, with frequent attacks on southern England. The kings of Wessex played a major role in resisting these attacks. Egbert defeated a joint Viking-Cornish army at Hingston Down in 838, and his son Aethelwulf defeated a Danish force at Aclea in 851. The latter's son Alfred was later to save Wessex by his efforts.

So, as we can see, the first incursions of the Scandinavians did not amount to invasion. From the early nuisance raids on northern England and Ireland in the 8th century, it was to be more than 70 years before the first full-scale Viking armies arrived. From the mid-ninth century the Vikings came not to plunder but to conquer and stay. Danish invaders took up winter quarters in Thanet in 850 and Sheppey in 854. The Danish 'great army' abandoned operations in northern France and overran East Anglia in 865 and Northumbria in 866-67.

In 865 a force of about 500 to 1,000 men landed in north-east England under the leadership of Ivar the Boneless, Ubbi and Halfden. These three men were sons of the unlikely-named Ragnar Hairy-Breeches, and were apparently seeking revenge for his death. Ragnar was reputed to have come to England with two ships some years earlier only to be roundly defeated by King Ella of Northumbria. Ella had Ragnar killed by throwing him into a pit of snakes. But before he died the Viking warned the Englishman that his sons would avenge him. He was right. In 867 the Danes defeated Ella at York and killed him. Gradually they overcame the little resistance they encountered in central and southern England. But the kingdom of Wessex was a different enemy altogether.

Wessex, which was attacked in 871, owed its survival in part to the skill of its young King Alfred, although the struggle was a desperate one and Wessex came very close to total defeat in 871 when the Danes won four of six major battles. Brief periods of peace came

at a price: Alfred's dealings with the Danes involved both the paying of tribute and the exchange of hostages. Wessex's resistance encouraged the Danes to turn to the conquest of Mercia. King Burgred fled to Rome in 874, and his successor Ceolwulf paid tribute to the Danes. In 877 Mercia east and north of Watling Street became Danish

Throughout these dramatic years, however, Alfred fought on. The young king incurred the wrath of the Vikings when, extraordinarily, he beat the them in a naval battle in 875, capturing one longship off the south coast and putting seven others to flight. It was the first time the invaders had found their sea power challenged and they determined to seek revenge. Hearing of Alfred's success, the Viking king Guthrum marched south with a large force and began the occupation of Wessex.

Most of the locals gave up their struggle against him but Alfred fought on as a resistance leader from a secret hideout in marshes at Athelney in the West Country. According to the Chronicle of the Kings of England, by William of Malmesbury:

'Alfred wished to find out the plans of the Viking army, so he disguised himself to look like a wandering minstrel and went boldly into their camp. He was able to get right into the innermost place where the Viking leaders were holding a council of war. There, playing his harp in a dark corner, he listened and looked as hard as he could and found out all their secret plans. He stayed in the camp several days until he was satisfied that he knew everything. Then he stole back to Athelney, gathered together all his leaders and explained to them how easily they could beat the Vikings.'

According to the Anglo-Saxon Chronicle, Alfred then:

'. . . rode to Egbert's Stone, east of Selwood, where he met all the people of Somerset, Wiltshire and Hampshire and they rejoiced to see him. And after one night he went to Iley and after another night to Edington and there fought against the whole Viking army and put it to flight.'

The Vikings were pursued to the Bristol Channel, where a peace treaty was drawn up at Edington, Wiltshire. Guthrum swore to leave the kingdom of Wessex in peace and even agreed to be baptised, with Alfred as his sponsor. Edington was a great victory for the English king and until his death in 899 he kept the invaders at bay throughout his lands (conquering London in 886). Alfred's successful opposition to these further sporadic Danish attacks enabled him to accumulate wealth and begin minting 'good pennies' — to historians, always a clear sign of a well-ordered kingdom!

Above Right: A modern sculpture of St Aidan, founder of the great monastery at Lindisfarne, he set up his outpost of Christianity on this remote stretch of the Northumberland coast in 635AD, following an invitation from King Oswald.

Far Right: A stained glass image of St Hilda, founder of Whitby Abbey, as she appears in the north-west window of Oxford Cathedral's Latin Chapel.

LINDISFARNE PRIORY

The monks of Lindisfarne were so successful at finding converts to Christianity in the North that they became rich and famous — too much so for their own good for they suffered a series of attacks over the centuries by those jealous of their success and wealth.

The Vikings were the first to attack in 793. Despite the isolated position of the place they called Holy Island, linked to the mainland by nothing more than a causeway, the monks were unable to repel them. They fled with their most precious possession, the one which attracted pilgrims from all parts: the body of St Cuthbert, at whose shrine miracles were performed.

Following the Viking destruction, it was 400 years before Lindisfarne was re-established, and it is the ruins of a mediaeval Benedictine priory that is seen today. The dramatic 'rainbow arch' over the nave of the priory church still stands. Nothing remains of the original monastery, which was founded in the seventh century by St Aidan, who became the first bishop of Lindisfarne in 635. Under him, Holy Island became known internationally as a centre of learning and culture. The Lindisfarne Gospels, now in the British Library, were copied and illuminated here in around 698. They are one of the finest examples of the skill and artistry of the early English monks.

A *view of the decorated pillars which adorn the nave at* Lindisfarne Priory church.

THE DANELAW: A COUNTRY DIVIDED

Despite King Alfred's success in keeping the Vikings out of his own kingdom of Wessex, a vast slice of the British Isles was now under their occupation. The Treaty of Edington, reported in the previous chapter, left the Danes with what became known as the Danelaw — that is, England east and north of a line from Chester to London.

Extensive Danish settlement is indicated by the large number of Scandinavian place-names ending in 'by' and 'throb' and, in the north-east today, by the many Scandinavian surnames ending in 'son'. The centre of Danelaw was Northumbria, while the Norwegians established a base at Dublin in 841 and in the first two decades of the tenth century colonised the coastline of north-west England, invading the Wirral from Dublin in 902. Scandinavian place-names are extensive in Cumbria and coastal Lancashire.

Meanwhile, a separate lifestyle continued in those parts of Britain not controlled by Danelaw. Freed from Viking insurgences, Alfred had turned to strengthening Wessex, building a fleet, creating a more effective system of military recruitment, and constructing a system of fortified towns. Existing towns had their walls restored or new ones constructed, while new burhs were established. It was a process that was continued by Alfred's successor Edward and by his daughter Aethelfled, who ruled English Mercia, the area south and west of Watling Street not settled by the Danes.

Defence under Alfred was followed by conquest under his heirs. Edward the Elder (899-924), Athelstan (924-39) and Edmund (939-46) conquered East Anglia, eastern Mercia and Yorkshire; the kings of Wessex brought modern England under their authority. Edward overran the Danish bases in eastern Mercia and built forts in the north-west Midlands, including Manchester (919) and Rhuddlan (921), to limit the danger of attack from the Norwegian kingdom of Dublin. The defeated Danes were allowed to keep their lands and the Danelaw retained distinctive features, including its own legal system.

English Mercia was absorbed by Wessex after the death of Aethelfled (918). In 923 the rulers of Scotland, Northumbria, Strathclyde and the Welsh kingdoms accepted Edward's lordship, giving the idea of a 'kingdom of Britain' some substance at last.

In 927 Athelstan captured York, in 934 he invaded Scotland, and in 937 he defeated a united army of Scots, Strathclyde Britons and Norsemen (Norwegians) from Ireland at Brunanburh. He formed alliances with leading continental rulers, fixed the Wye as the boundary with South Wales and restricted Cornish power to west of the Tamar. Despite formidable resistance from the Yorkshire Danes, they were finally reduced — Eric Bloodaxe, their last king, being killed in an ambush in 954.

The areas reconquered from the Danes were quick to abandon their old gods and to adopt Christianity. Ultimately it was their conversion to Christianity which ended the Vikings' warlike habits and turned them into more peaceable farmers and sea traders.

Their conquering reign had lasted little more than 300 years but in that time they bequeathed much more to Western Europe than savagery and brutality. Their burning desire to explore the world made them truly the lords of the sea — an inheritance which, by their knowledge of shipbuilding and navigation, they bequeathed to Britain, thus shaping that emerging nation's great naval tradition.

England was now making remarkably swift progress in political and social terms. Royal authority had been re-established under an expanding state ruled by the house of Wessex. A county or shire system extended into areas reconquered from the Danes. The shires were in turn divided into hundreds and, in Scandinavian areas, wapen-takes, responsible for maintaining law and order. Their public courts were a link between rulers and the fairly numerous free groups in society. The coinage was improved, with 70 mints set up around the country, with a flexible rate of exchange boosting foreign trade. There was also a system of assessment for taxation and military service based on hides, the hide being the amount of land deemed necessary to support a peasant family.

The church made sure that it was closely linked with royalty, and an ecclesiastical revival took place that was largely monastic in inspiration. Following the decay of monastic life in the ninth century, Edmund's son Edgar (959-75) reformed the monasteries, and Canterbury, Sherborne, Winchester and Worcester all became monastic cathedrals.

The church was well endowed (the total income of monasteries and nunneries by the early eleventh century was far greater than that of the king). The Anglo-Saxon church had long provided missionaries, such as Boniface and Willibrord, to help convert Germany and the Low Countries to Christianity, a sign of the vitality of English Christianity. It sent others to Scandinavia in the late tenth and early eleventh centuries. This religious revival provided a literary and cultural activity which revealed itself in brilliant manuscript illumination, stone carving and embroidery.

The kingdom of Wessex had by now become what was later termed the 'Old English Monarchy'. This state was still very much centred on Wessex, Athelstan alone among the tenth-century rulers spending much time in Mercia. Wessex was administered from its four heartland shires of Hampshire, Wiltshire, Dorset and Somerset

Opposite: *The ruins of St Augustine's Abbey, Canterbury, founded in 598AD as a shrine for burying the kings and archbishops of Kent. There was further large-scale building on the site for the next four centuries, although much was demolished in 1070 to make way for Abbot Scotland's great Norman Abbey.*

the regions where the kings spent most of their time. However, the precariousness of nationhood was indicated in 957 when the Mercians and Northumbrians renounced allegiance to Eadwig in favour of his brother Edgar. The schism was healed, although Edgar also became king of Wessex on Eadwig's death in 959. The allegiance of Northumbria to whomever ruled at Winchester remained uncertain until well into the eleventh century.

The country prospered, however. As a result of agricultural advances and the production of wool and cloth, England became wealthy by the standards of contemporary northern Europe, and a tempting prize to foreign rulers. The power of the old English monarchy was displayed in 973 when other British rulers made a formal submission to King Edgar at Chester. The Winchester monk and chronicler Aelfric wrote:

'. . . King Edgar
furthered Christianity, and built many monasteries,
and his kingdom still continued in peace,
so that no fleet was heard of,
save that of the people themselves who held this land;
and all the kings of the Cymry and the Scots
that were in this island, came to Edgar
once upon a day, being eight kings,
and they all bowed themselves to Edgar's rule.'

The peace and unity of England was not to survive Edgar's death in 975. Both his sons were young. The elder, Edward, succeeded but was unpopular and was murdered in 978 by supporters of the younger son, Aethelred 'the Unready' (978-1016). Aethelred has been the subject of scorn throughout history, not least because of the hostile tone of the Anglo Saxon Chronicle. In fact Aethelred made major efforts to improve the state's defences but he lacked the presence and natural authority to command or elicit trust. This limited his ability to deal with the next crisis to hit the British Isles — the return of the Vikings.

England under the recent kings of Wessex, Scotland under its outstanding ninth-century ruler Kenneth MacAlpin and much of Wales under the rulers of Gwynedd, had all experienced a welcome measure of statehood. But so too had the Viking lands — enabling them again to organise themselves into larger armies.

Soon after Aethelred's accession, the Danes started mounting major attacks, in one of which they defeated the Essex militia under ealdorman Brihtnoth at Maldon (991). Aethelred used a mixture of bribes (Danegeld) and violence, such as a pitiless massacre of English-resident Danes in 1002 to maintain his power. The Danes retaliated with fearsome vengeance over a decade and in 1013 resistance collapsed. The following year Aethelred was briefly driven into exile in Normandy by King Sweyn of Denmark, who was recognised but never crowned as king of England.

Aethelred returned on Sweyn's death. But the struggle was continued by Sweyn's son, Cnut, while resistance was hampered by divisions among the English, especially that between Aethelred and his eldest son, the energetic Edmund Ironside. After Aethelred's death, England was divided between Cnut and Edmund in 1016 by the Peace of Alney, Cnut receiving Mercia and Northumbria. Edmund, however, died and Cnut became King of all England from 1016-35.

England was now, almost by default, part of a greater Scandinavian empire. Cnut, following the death of his older broth-

er Harold, had also become king of Denmark and thereby the newly conquered Norway. The Vikings now largely ruled the western seaboard of Europe including, significantly, Normandy which still bears their name as 'home of the northmen'.

Cnut chose to rule these dominions from England, where he largely followed the peaceable practices of the local kings of Wessex, although he introduced a number of Danes into the aristocracy and divided the kingdom into a small number of earldoms. The earldom of Wessex was given to Godwin, an English protege of Cnut, who married a Danish princess and gave Danish names to four of his six sons, including Harold. An Anglo-Viking aristocracy was being created, as England looked increasingly overseas to the lands of her Scandinavian conquerors.

But for the most extraordinary catalogue of events that were to follow, the British Isles might have developed as the centre of a Viking empire.

Above and Right: Two views of Whitby Abbey in North Yorkshire. The original structure was founded by St Hilda in 657AD but its proximity to the north-east coast made it an easy target for the Vikings, who destroyed it in 867. It was re-built as a Benedictine house in 1078 although today's ruins are the remnants of a later 13th and 14th century design.

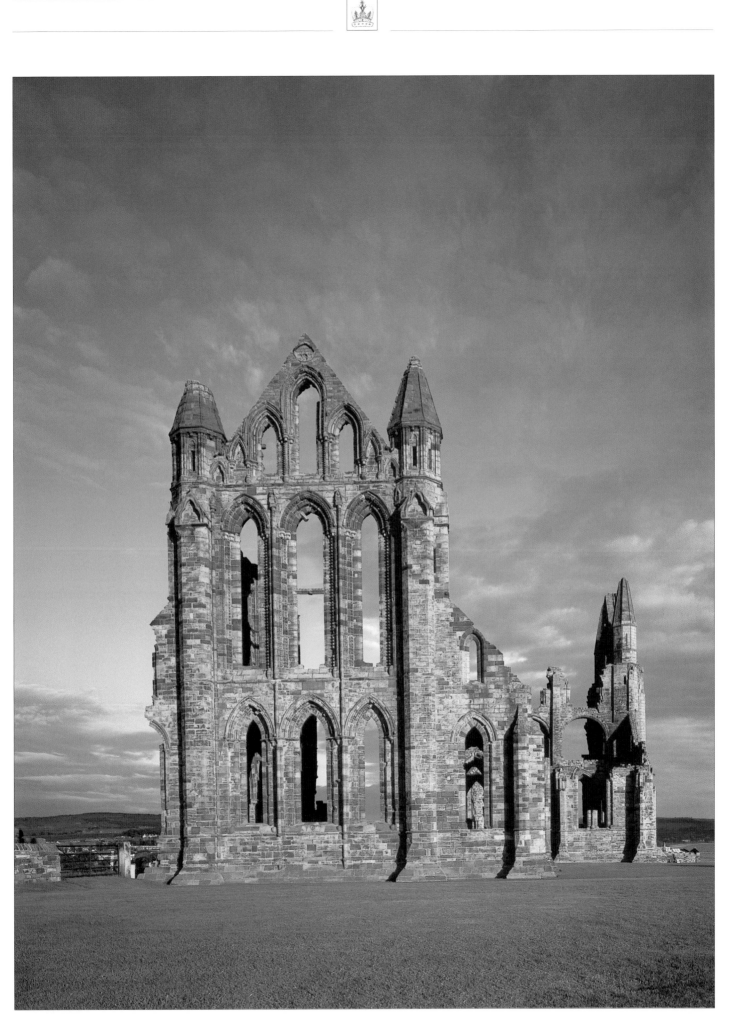

THE NORMAN
CONQUEST

Edward 'the Confessor' had spent 25 years in exile as a refugee from the Vikings in Normandy before his popularly acclaimed return to England in 1042. Following the reigns of Cnut's sons, Harold and Harthacnut, the ancient house of Wessex was now restored. Edward's reign, although brief, was prosperous for Britain — but it was overshadowed by the problem of the succession.

When Edward died childless on 5 January 1066 the Witan, the great council of the realm, elected as their king Harold Godwinson, Earl of Wessex, who claimed that Edward had made him a deathbed promise of the throne. The largest landowner in the country, Harold had acquired considerable prestige from successful campaigns against Gruffydd ap Llywelyn, King of Gwynedd, who had conquered all of Wales and sacked Hereford in 1055. At Rhuddlan in 1063 Harold defeated Gruffydd, who was soon after murdered by his followers, his head being sent to Harold. The next threat to the peace of England was to come from Scandinavia, where the Vikings were again casting greedy eyes upon the British Isles. In these dangerous times, Harold, the popular war hero, was seen as the one man whose prowess in battle could maintain the unity of England.

Having vanquished the Welsh, and fearing invasion by Vikings from the north, King Harold came to the throne facing yet another threat from a third quarter. Duke William of Normandy, the head of a warlike people descended from Viking settlers, laid claim to the English succession — on the faint grounds that he was the late King Edward the Confessor's illegitimate second cousin once removed. However, he alleged that, when visiting Edward in 1051, the old king had solemnly promised the throne to him. And, with a strong army assembled on the Norman side of the English Channel, he was out to get it. That he managed to do so was only down to a series of extraordinarily unlucky breaks for King Harold…

To thwart any invasion by William, Harold initially concentrated his forces along the south coast. When bad weather prevented William from sailing in September 1066, Harold disbanded his forces and left for London. There he heard that the Norwegians under Harold Hardrada, King of Norway, had landed in Yorkshire. They defeated the local earls at Gate Fulford on 20 September and seized York, winning a measure of local support. King Harold and his men were now called upon to perform an unparalleled feat in military history.

• On 18 September he learned of the Yorkshire landings.

• Harold marched his army north at miraculous speed.

• On 25 September he decimated the Norwegians at Stamford Bridge. Hardrada was slain and his defeated army needed only twenty ships of the invasion force of 300 to ferry the survivors home.

• Then to his horror, Harold heard that the Normans had landed at Pevensey, Sussex, on 28 September.

Above: *A reconstruction of the most famous battle ever fought on English soil — the 1066 Battle of Hastings. The engagement was dominated by the Normans' skilful use of archery, supported by cavalry charge, which effectively broke up King Harold II's massed infantry. Both sides suffered heavy losses but Harold's death, allowed William, Duke of Normandy to claim the English throne.*

Right: *The Great Gatehouse at Battle Abbey, near Hastings. The Benedictine Abbey was founded by William in 1067 to celebrate his victory and offer prayers for the souls of the fallen. He ordered that the high altar be placed on the precise spot where King Harold fell.*

• He force-marched his men back to London, recruited fresh soldiers and arrived in the deep Weald of Sussex on the night of 13 October — an astonishing 250 miles in all.

• At 9am the following morning, the Normans, after two weeks' preparation, joined them in battle.

What really happened on 14 October 1066, the most celebrated date in English history? Myth and legend have clouded the dramatic reality of the conflict. But the truth, as we now know it, is more amazing than any fiction.

At nine o'clock that Saturday morning, two armies were drawn up in the Sussex countryside. That led by Harold Godwinson was utterly exhausted — 5,000 men weakened by battle and fatigue after their victory in the north and their astonishing march south. William's Norman army of 7,000 men were fresh from an easy Channel crossing. Apart from the difference in preparedness, there was one other crucial difference between the two armies. Norman

cavalry fought on horseback, wielding swords and thrusting lances. Those of the English who rode to battle dismounted and fought on foot.

The English line, a dozen close-packed ranks of infantry and archers, were drawn up on Senlac Hill, just ouside of the town of Battle which subsequently grew on the site. In the centre stood Harold, surrounded by his 'housecarls', an elite bodyguard of crack troops, the best in Europe and wielding the dreaded two-handed battleaxe.

William attacked first. His infantry, many of them mercenaries, made little impact against the brave and unbudging English. They retreated in disarray, passing the word that the day was lost and that William himself had been killed. The English soldiers were jubilant. With equal vigour, they beat off an awesome Norman cavalry charge which followed.

Then came the error that changed the course of the battle and English history.

Repulsed, the Norman knights turned back to regroup — a manoeuvre that appeared to the English to be a disorderly retreat. The front lines of the Saxon army broke ranks and charged down Senlac Hill in pursuit of the horsemen. William saw his chance and staged a further series of feigned flights, successfully enticing his enemy to break ranks. Depleted, King Harold's army reformed — 'withstanding as though rooted to the soil', according to one chronicler. But there were now too few of them. Harold had foolishly arrived in Sussex ahead of the reserves (the fyrd, a sort of Territorial Army) whom he had recruited in London.

The final push came as dusk fell. The professional Norman archers, using short or 'Danish' bows, advanced to within 100 yards of the English, as they had done throughout the day. Attacking uphill, they fired their showers of arrows high into the air. It was this hellish hail of death that brought the collapse of the English army.

King Harold was struck in or near the eye — wounding though not killing him — as so graphically depicted in the Bayeux Tapestry. As he desperately tried to pull the arrow out of his head, a few rampaging Norman knights came upon him and cut him

down with their swords. The disintegrating English fled, with William himself in pursuit on his fourth horse of the day, the previous three having been killed beneath him. The fyrds arrived six hours later — far too late to turn the tide of war.

As penance for the dreadful slaughter of that day, the newly-proclaimed William I of England built an abbey on the site of the battle. He placed the high altar on the very spot where his noble adversary Harold had fallen.

In a way, the unification of England under the house of Wessex ensured that it fell rapidly to William the Conqueror — unlike the more lengthy processes by which the Iron Age and Romano-British kingdoms had fallen to Rome and the Anglo-Saxons. Following his victory at the Battle of Hastings, the victorious William crossed the Thames to the west of London and, as he approached the city, morale among the defendants crumbled. At Berkhampstead they submitted to William. And on Christmas day he was acclaimed king in Westminster Abbey.

At last, some stability was coming to England. The Normans recognised that although the country they had conquered was wealthy, a proper administrative system had to be established to ensure future prosperity.

Indeed, it became a time of great power building by a people who were basically warriors. Castles were built to emphasise the Norman presence and authority. These were initially earth and timber constructions which could be quickly erected in areas where defence was considered of immediate importance. These later gave way to mightier and more permanent stone castles such as the White Tower in London and Windsor Castle. Stone cathedrals soon dotted the landscape too, and again, those such as Durham cathedral are testimony to Norman architectural skills. All such buildings were evidence of the conquerors' control, providing centres for both political and religious rule.

Now, too, came the beginnings of a defined social structure, with Norman lords the masters and lower orders very much their servants. Creating what was to become known historically as the feudal system, the lords pledged support and protection of their people and provided them with land in return for service — principally military service. For the understanding was that this 'military tenancy' meant Norman lords were obligated to provide a number of knights for service roughly proportionate to the size of their estate.

At this time in English history, the island's boundaries were becoming more defined, with an area to the east and south and the highland ranges of Wales and Scotland being drawn up to come under written administration. Despite the teething problems of feudalism, newly introduced laws, higher taxes and different tongues, the nation slowly became unified.

Left: *The large Norman motte and bailey of Berkhamsted Castle in Hertfordshire. The earliest work was begun by William the Conqueror's half-brother, Robert of Mortain.*

Above Right: *Stonework at Dover Castle, one of England's largest and best-preserved fortresses.*

Below Right: *The Tower of London by floodlight. In its time it became the most feared — and the most famous — prison in England. The central White Tower was built by William the Conqueror around 1080.*

But while the common people adapted to their servitude, the Norman hierarchy fought amongst themselves. Nobles and monarchs wanted more power and land. Inheritance was almost always disputed, leading to the establishing of a rule under which the eldest male child automatically enjoyed a rightful claim. Even this was not without its problems. William I (1066-87) died after being thrown from his horse in the French town of Mantes which he had burnt as a result of a border conflict. William left Normandy to his eldest son Robert and England to his second son William II, believing that he was the right man to rule an often troublesome country. Robert, however, wanted to be lord of both nations. He and William, known as Rufus (1087-1100) because of his red hair, became bitter foes. Eventually Robert resigned Normandy to William in 1096 in order to raise funds to embark on the First Crusade.

William had an impressive military record. In 1092 he took an army to Cumbria which, although in the hands of an English family, had Malcolm III of Scotland as its recognised overlord. William created a town and built a castle at Carlisle, established a Norman ally at Kendal and made the Solway and the Liddel the northern border of his kingdom. He was also successful against Norman rebels and the French. But William earned a reputation not only as a fine soldier but the patron of fine buildings too. His greatest achievement was Westminster Hall,whose vast interior is still used on state occasion.

William died in 1100, in what some say was a suspicious hunting accident in the New Forest, while out with his brother Henry.

Henry I moved quickly to secure power and eventually defeated older brother Robert at Tinchebrai (Normandy) in 1106. Robert was imprisoned in Cardiff where he died in 1134.

Henry was not a man with whom to come into conflict. Those who crossed him were subjected to appalling torture. Anyone, for instance, considered responsible for irregularities in minting money was blinded and castrated. It was his tight administration of the currency that laid the groundwork for today's exchequer (named after the chequer or chess board).

The wars Henry was forced to wage in Normandy were a considerable drain on his resources — he was significantly poorer than Rufus had been — but this was compensated for by his efficient management. Henry was also respected more by the church than his brother - despite talk of siring more than 20 children, only two of whom were legitimate. His only legitimate son, William, died at sea in 1119.

But the Norman kings, like their Anglo-Saxon predecessors, worked closely with the church and the fervently supported the reforming Popes of the late eleventh century. New religious orders were introduced to England, previously home only to Benedictine houses, the sole monastic order in Saxon England. First came the Cluniac order from Burgundy, then the Augustinian priories, with groups of canons (priests who lived together under a common rule). These orders were later joined by the solitary Cistercians, who founded the famous abbey at Tintern.

Henry I married Matilda, daughter of Malcolm III of Scotland, in 1100. By 1107, his throne was finally secure. With his brother incarcerated at Devizes and a victory over the church to appoint his own bishops, the king felt a confident ruler. He had also sealed a treaty with Archbishop Anselm of Canterbury under which bishops must pay homage to Henry for the estates that accompanied their office. The deal ended the feuding which began under William and gained Henry the support of the Pope.

Henry I died in France in 1135 from food poisoning, after gorg-

Above: *The distinctive outline of Carisbrooke Castle, on the Isle of Wight. The fortress is of mostly 13th century construction, although considerable improvements to the defences were made by Elizabeth I to ward off invasion. Charles I had the dubious pleasure of being imprisoned here in 1647/48.*

Right: *Only the great square keep survives intact at Rochester Castle, Kent. The castle was once the largest and most luxurious in Britain, containing a magnificent great hall within its merged second and third storeys.*

ing on lamprey fish. Only one child, his illegitimate son Robert, Earl of Gloucester, was at his deathbed. Because his only legitimate son was dead, Henry left behind him a disputed inheritance. His daughter Matilda had married Geoffrey Plantagenet, Count of Anjou, in 1128. Her father's death made Matilda and her husband rightful rulers of England. But Geoffrey, at war with Normandy, was never to set foot in England.

So, far from uniting the kingdoms of England and Anjou, Henry's death led to twenty years of destructive civil war. Matilda, despite her husband's detachment, was determined to take the throne — and one man was equally determined she should not. As soon as he heard of Henry's death, his nephew Stephen of Blois, son of William the I's daughter Adela, sailed from Boulogne to seize power.and was crowned by a reluctant Archbishop of Canterbury. Ironically, the woman Stephen chose as his queen was also called Matilda.

The period of his reign is known as 'the anarchy' when 'Christ and his angels slept.' And not without good reason. Stephen was

recrowned king in 1141 after an astonishing year which had seen him defeated, captured, deposed and finally victorious.

In February that year, while he was besieging the rebellious Earl 'Moustaches' Ranulf of Chester in Lincoln Castle, he was overwhelmed by the superior forces of Matilda, led by her half-brother Robert of Gloucester. Refusing to flee, Stephen fought until he was captured. He was held in Robert of Gloucester's castle while Matilda made her way to London to seek the succession. But the citizens of London, already wary of her, became hostile when she demanded large sums of money from them. While preparing for her coronation, the Londoners rose and drove her out. Stephen's supporters, led by his wife, defeated her army outside Winchester and captured Robert of Gloucester. He was exchanged for Stephen who once again sat on the throne. In 1148, Matilda left England and returned to her husband in Normandy, dropping her claim to the throne.

King Stephen died in 1154, two years after his beloved wife. The question of succession had been resolved only a year earlier,when Stephen had dramatically disinherited his son. Eustace, in favour of Henry Plantagenet — son of his old adversary and thwarted claimant to the throne, Matilda. A new royal house now had the task of trying to end England's anarchy.

Below: *The massive keep of Castle Rising, in Norfolk, was built in 1138 by William de Albini, Earl of Lincoln in the same year that he married Henry I's widow Queen Alice. The castle's Norman earthwork defences are unusually well preserved.*

Opposite: *A splendid aerial view of Dover Castle – the 'Gateway to England'. Dover Castle is possibly the most important fortress in England. The Romans knew its strategic value and so did the Conqueror who, on defeating Harold at Hastings, made straight for Dover. He built a motte-and-bailey castle in, it is said, only eight days. Only when his crossing point with France was secure did he continue his march into the heartland of England.*

The crowning of King Henry II in 1154 healed the rift between England's royal rivals, Stephen and Matilda. Henry was the son of Matilda. The death of Eustace, son and heir to Stephen, paved the way for a compromise deal in which Henry took the throne. Stephen's second son William was paid off handsomely with large tracts of land. Henry's father was Geoffrey Plantagenet, Count of Anjou, and the dynasty became known as the Plantagenets.

Although king of England, Henry was much concerned with matters in France. After all, he was born in Le Mans, did not visit England until he was nine years old and was to eventually die in France, in Chinon. His queen was Eleanor of Aquitaine, a union which brought vast new lands to the south of this dual nation. Henry certainly had his work cut out. There were troublesome Scots to contend with as well as brooding Celts and greedy and unpredictable barons from the Scottish borders to the Pyrenees. Energetically, he tackled the challenges that dogged his reign.

Yet his 'new broom sweeps clean' approach, which undoubtedly helped restore some semblance of order to England, is largely forgotten by history. Henry is remembered as the king responsible for the death of St Thomas Becket.

Becket was the son of a London merchant, who rose to become Chancellor to the king and later Archbishop of Canterbury. Henry was convinced he had a tame churchman in the form of Becket, who was a personal friend. On that count, the appointment suited Henry well as he was aiming to reduce the power of the church. He wanted an end to the system in which the church punished its own, often more leniently than would a civil court. Likewise, appeals to Rome, Henry felt, flew in the face of his own authority and should be scrapped.

Henry's spearhead into the church was known as the Constitutions of Clarendon of 1164 and contained 15 points. There Becket and his bishops fought the proposals for two days before caving in. Almost immediately Becket regretted his decision and stood once again for the interests of the church, in opposition to the king. Henry had Becket arrested and in 1165 the country's most eminent churchman fled into exile. It was five years before he returned to England to resume his battle of wills with Henry.

In a fit of outrage at his court in Normandy, Henry burst out: 'Will no one rid me of this turbulent priest?' In response, four knights made their way to England, found Becket in Canterbury Cathedral and on 29 December 1170 slayed him with their swords.

Henry was grief-stricken when he heard about the killing. He donned sackcloth and ashes and loud lamentations were heard from behind the door of his chamber, where he imprisoned himself for three days. Three years after his death, Becket was canonised. A year after that Henry had monks flog him in the street as a mark of his repentance, although he always maintained that he had never ordered the killing.

If Henry believed his worst enemies were abroad, he was sadly mistaken. In the last years of his life, his wife and three of his four sons plotted against him. Eleanor slaughtered the king's mistress, 'Fair' Rosamund Clifford, and was so disagreeable that she was eventually imprisoned.

When his eldest son, also called Henry, was crowned successor in 1169, his second son Richard was incensed. By a coincidental quirk both later joined forces with Philip II of France and waged war on their father. John, Henry's favourite son, joined them. By now both Henry the Younger and Geoffrey, Henry's other son, were dead. The aggressors compelled a heartbroken King Henry to accept a shamefully humiliating peace. A month later he died.

Richard was crowned king of England on 3 September 1189 in Westminster. It was one of the few occasions he visited the country during his reign. It is calculated that during a decade of rule he spent less than a year with his feet on English soil.

Nor was it the happy occasion he might have wished. By his own decree, Jews were banned from the coronation. When some turned up they were attacked by Richard's courtiers. Many were killed and those released were badly injured. The incident sparked a pogrom in London and Jews were rooted out and slaughtered by the score.

Richard, despite his foreign travels, was a popular king. His upbringing at the court in Poitiers, France, with its emphasis on chivalry and knightly courage, served him well. He won the name 'Lionheart' — although whether his personal integrity matched up to his bravery is open to question.

It was the lure of the Third Crusade that took Richard overseas. Jerusalem, the centre of Christianity, was once again under control of Muslims led by the charismatic Saladin. Prompted by attacks on pilgrims, the Pope sanctioned another Crusade.

Richard stayed in England long enough to raise taxes to pay for the expedition. He jokingly said that he would have sold London if only he could have found a buyer. In 1190 he set off for the Holy Land with his old ally, Philip II of France. Their relationship was soured, however, when Richard failed to marry Philip's sister Alice as promised. Instead Richard wed Berengaria of Navarre, the choice of his mother Eleanor.

Deserted by Philip, Richard fought on and delivered a brutally decisive blow to the Saracens at Acre. Now he fell out with Duke Leopold of Austria over the spoils of victory and the Duke withdrew from the Crusade. Wisely, Richard negotiated with Saladin when he arrived at Jerusalem. The two men got along famously and

Right: *A fine 14th century oriel, or windowed recess, is the splendour of Prudhoe Castle in Northumberland, which also has its gatehouse, curtain wall and keep.*

agreed that pilgrims had a right of entry to the Holy City while the Muslims remained in charge.

Returning from Palestine, Richard was captured by the irate Duke Leopold and held to ransom for more than a year. At home his ambitious brother John was in league with the disgruntled Philip. Both undoubtedly contemplated abandoning Richard to Duke Leopold but decided the repercussions would be too great. As a result of the collusion between Philip and John, further English territory was lost. Richard went to war in Europe to try to redress the losses. But in 1199, in a siege of the castle of Chalus, near Limousin — so minor an engagement that he did not even bother to don his armour — Richard was hit in the shoulder by a crossbow bolt. The wound festered and he died.

Richard's younger brother John succeeded him to the throne. King John has long been cast as the arch villain of English monarchs. Under scrutiny, there seems little to recommend the man who connived against his father, King Henry, even though he was the favourite son, tried to usurp his brother, Richard, and according to rumour did away with his nephew, Prince Arthur, who had a legitimate claim on the throne. Treacherous, impetuous, foolish and unwise, John found a capacity to alienate one and all. Before his succession in 1199, he had been sent to Ireland by his father to rule. He and his companion rudely laughed aloud at the beards worn by the Irish chieftains who came to pay homage to him.

His rule there was a disaster. John, like his brother before him, fell out with Philip of France and lost many further English possessions on the Continent in the ensuing conflict. In a bid to fund the war against Philip, John taxed his people mercilessly. Perhaps that is how the tale of folk hero Robin Hood sprang up. The legend of someone who stole from the rich to give to the poor — who were becoming still poorer thanks to the greedy king — was an irresistible one. Still, there is scant evidence to suggest that the legend of a virtuous Robin Hood is anything other than folklore.

Sensationally, John rowed with Pope Innocent III by refusing to sanction Rome's appointee to the archbishopric of Canterbury; instead John nominated his own candidate. In 1208 the Pope placed all of England under an interdict, cutting off the entire country from the church. The dead were buried in unconsecrated ground while

Above: *Henry II is believed to have added the dominating great keep to the existing structure of Richmond Castle which lies above the River Swale in North Yorkshire. Although the castle fell to ruin after the 16th century the keep with its magnificent archway remains almost intact.*

Right: *The remains of Clun Castle on the Welsh borders are dominated by a ruined keep and a pair of 13th century towers.*

Mass was banned. The following year the King himself was excommunicated. Only when Philip II of France was poised to invade did John make his peace with the Pope. He effectively bought his way back into favour.

John's row with the powerful English barons left the most enduring legacy. With barons in the north and east poised to revolt, John was pressured into signing the Magna Carta, or Great Charter. Much later the Magna Carta was hailed as a statement of civil rights. It was not. The campaigning barons cared as little for the plight of the common man as the king himself.

The Magna Carta defined the role of the barons in government, limited royal powers and set out the spheres of power of the English church. Prime among its purposes was to declare that no one — not even the monarch — was above the law.

Yet the 39th article of the charter is perhaps responsible for its progressive reputation. It reads: 'No free man shall be arrested or imprisoned or dispossessed or outlawed or harmed in any way save by the lawful judgment of his equals under the law of the land. Justice will not be sold to any man nor will it be refused or delayed.' And so the Magna Carta, signed at Runnymede, near Windsor, Berkshire, in 1215, became one of the cornerstones of British justice. It was restated several times in later years.

When John reneged on his Charter signature later that same year, he sparked the first Barons' War. Outraged barons offered the English Crown to the future King Louis VIII of France who attempted an invasion.

At the height of the conflict, John died in agony at Newark-on-Trent Castle, in Nottinghamshire. The theory that he was poisoned has been largely discredited. He died in grief, days after his baggage train was tragically lost in quicksand while crossing The Wash.

Above: *When Henry II built Orford Castle in Suffolk in 1165 it was a state-of-the-art design with no fewer than 18 sides to defend. The number of sides was crucial in defeating the commonly used enemy tactic of undermining the corner of a beseiged castle.*

Right: *Conisborough Castle in Yorkshire was built by Hamelin Plantagenet, half-brother to Henry II, and features one of the first round keeps ever built in Britain.*

Arundel Castle was originally built by the Normans in the early 11th century, Henry II built much of the stone castle in 1176 - 89. From the 13th century the castle has mainly been in the hands of the Earls of Arundel, and from 1580 the Dukes of Norfolk.

THE MEDIEVAL PERIOD

With the death of John in 1216, his son, the boy-king Henry III, came to the throne with a coronation held at what is now Gloucester Cathedral. Although only nine years of age, he was an acceptable royal figurehead. Accordingly, the warring barons rallied to drive the invading French King Louis from English shores.

Hubert de Burgh was among Henry's loyal regents (or 'Protectors') and it was he who secured a damning victory against the French at sea off the Kent coast at Sandwich — by bizarre means. Powdered lime was tossed into the eyes of the French sailors, blinding them at the height of the battle. Another victory on land at Lincoln dispatched the French and from 1217 there was peace between the two countries.

In effect, it wasn't until 1232 that Henry was able to assume full control of his country. One of his first acts was to rid himself of the loyal de Burgh by placing him under arrest. Hubert escaped from prison and sought sanctuary in the parish church at Devizes. It was customary to grant the right of asylum to those in the boundaries of a church. Hubert was nonetheless dragged from the church and returned to gaol. Furious, the Bishop of Salisbury intervened and insisted he was taken back to the sanctuary of the church. The king's men had the place surrounded until de Burgh's supporters stormed it to rescue him.

Henry's reign was long but not particularly distinguished. There was a series of disastrous wars in France as he set about trying to recoup territories lost by his father. At home there was some shameful anti-Semitism which would escalate until Jews were finally expelled from England in 1290 by Henry's son Edward I.

On a more positive note, there was the arrival of spectacles during the 12th century, a tremendous benefit to those elite men of letters. Universities were founded at Oxford and Cambridge and the studies of science and medicine began in earnest. Henry did much to refurbish Westminster Abbey, work which he carried out as a tribute to his personal hero, St Edward the Confessor.

The ineptitude of Henry III and his corrupt advisors inspired the wrath of some barons. The king's own brother-in-law, Simon de Montfort, led a rebellion which began successfully enough. De Montfort's army, entirely English-based, routed the king's forces at Lewes in Sussex on 14 May 1264. Lining up for the royalists were a significant number of foreign mercenaries as well as Henry's brother Richard of Cornwall and his son Edward.

Edward, a commanding figure, displayed some of the military flair which would later earn him respect as a warrior king. He was 1.8m (6ft 2in tall) — which earned him the nick-name 'Longshanks' — and physically fit. Incensed by the rebels, he pursued them for miles. But in his absence, de Montfort captured Richard and ultimately Henry and Edward.

De Montfort had ideas ahead of his time about a Great Council

Above: *The flip side of a penny from the reign of King Edward I, now housed in the Lindisfarne Priory Museum.*

Opposite: *Berkeley Castle, Gloucestershire. The original castle was built by William FitzOsbern shortly after the battle of Hastings. In the 12th century Robert Fitzharding received permission to build a castle of stone and the Berkeleys are his decendants. Edward II is said to have been murdered horribly here – by having a red hot poker inserted into his nether regions.*

or Parliament with members drawn from all over England. However, his choice of representative was irksome to the barons. The thuggish behaviour of some of his supporters worried them even more. Overseas, a Royalist rescue mission was being summoned. At this point, key figures in the civil war switched sides, leaving de Montfort with seriously depleted ranks.

Edward escaped from captivity after persuading his guards that he should race each of their horses in turn to see which was the fastest. After driving the animals hard Edward suddenly leapt on to a fresh steed and galloped away, leaving the frustrated guards with horses too weary to make chase.

A vengeful Edward confronted Simon de Montfort in battle at Evesham in August 1265 and secured the freedom of his father and a decisive victory. During the battle de Montfort was killed and his head severed, to be displayed on a pike by way of warning to other prospective insurgents. The battle also claimed the lives of 18 barons, 160 knights and 4,000 soldiers.

As peace returned to England, it was Edward who was king in all but name. When Henry died in 1272 Edward was fighting a Crusade. So confident was he about the security of his tenure on the throne that he did not return for two years for his coronation.

Although firm to the point of cruelty, Edward was a rational man with patience, foresight and fortitude. On a personal level he was a devout Christian and a devoted husband to his Queen, Eleanor of Castile. Just a decade after de Montfort, he instituted the Great Council with two representatives drawn from each borough. Ironically, the chosen representatives were so reluctant to appear that they had to be threatened with fines in order to ensure their attendance.

Edward was determined to quell rebellion among the Welsh and the Scots. His main adversary in Wales was Llewelyn ap Griffith, who called himself the Prince of Wales, although his sphere of influence was in fact restricted to Caernarfon, Anglesey, Merioneth and part of Denbigh. After Llewelyn refused to pay homage to Edward following his coronation, Edward replied by seizing his bride-to-be, Eleanor, daughter of Simon de Montfort.

In 1276 Edward followed up with an invasion. Llewelyn was beaten back into the Snowdonia mountains and was starved into submission. A shaky peace came into force but within four years Llewelyn had been killed in a border skirmish. His duplicitous brother Dafydd, who at one time supported the English, was hanged by Edward as a traitor. From the Welsh wars came Caernarfon Castle, one of a string of fortresses built to subdue the Welsh. It was at this imposing castle that Edward's son and successor was born. The baby, also called Edward, was publicly declared Prince of Wales.

Edward fared less well on the northern borders, where the Scots refused to submit. When the Scottish throne fell vacant, Edward was asked to pick one of 12 claimants. John Balliol was chosen as the incumbent. Although Balliol began by paying homage to Edward, he was soon moved to rebellion — providing Edward with the excuse he'd been eagerly awaiting — to invade. In 1296 he won the victory he craved and contemptuously removed the Stone of Destiny, the Scottish coronation stone of Scone, to London.

An uprising two years later was suppressed with the same ruthless efficiency. But still the rumblings of rebellion swept through the glens. Edward had yet to face the most successful of his Scottish foes, Robert the Bruce.

A campaign against the English by Bruce got off to a faltering start. He blundered badly by stabbing an eminent rival in a church at Dumfries. After the Red Comyn died at Bruce's hand, Edward and the Pope were united in anger at such a violation of the church's sanctity. Still, Bruce was crowned by the bishop of St Andrews.

A first conflict with the English and the furious Comyn clan left Bruce reeling. However, as he pondered his plight in hiding, he watched a spider try, try and try again to build a web. According to fable, this humble sight inspired him to renew his efforts. In 1307 he prepared for battle. Edward, now 68 and close to death, travelled to meet him. The English king failed to make the battlefield, dying in Burgh by Sands, Cumbria.

Edward wanted his bones carried before his army until Scotland was won. This was impractical. Instead his body was taken to Waltham Abbey and finally to Westminster Abbey where he was laid close to St Edward the Confessor. His tomb was inscribed, according to his instructions, with the words 'Scottorum malleus' — hammer of the Scots. It was a defiant but not entirely accurate tribute.

It was Edward's deathbed wish to have his 23-year-old son continue the fight. Yet he must have known in his heart of heart's that this would not and could not happen. Edward II was a pleasure-loving homosexual, as feeble as his father was bold. His father was a hard act to follow, and perhaps Edward II's downfall was that he inherited none of the soldierly bearing that was a prerequisite of kingship in those days.

The new king was less concerned with Scotland than he was with the fate of his favourite companion, Piers Gaveston. Edward I had insisted the snide Gaveston was banished. Now Gaveston could be reinstated, much to the fury of the barons. They loathed him and were deeply suspicious of the amateur theatre which delighted both Gaveston and Edward II. In 1312 Edward's close companion was seized by some of England's most notable earls, sentenced to death by a kangaroo court and hanged at Blacklow Hill in Warwickshire.

Matters went from bad to worse for Edward. It was 1314 before he found the enthusiasm to march on Scotland. He went north with a large army but found himself outmanoeuvred at every turn. The Scottish victory at Bannockburn ensured independence from England, and a fiery new nation with Robert the Bruce (Robert I) at its helm.

Despite his sexual preferences, Edward had married a French noblewoman, Isabella, and sired four children. She grew to hate him, however, and fled to France where she plotted with her lover, the rebel baron Roger Mortimer, to oust Edward.

After they landed in Suffolk in 1327 they gathered popular support. From behind the walls of Kenilworth Castle, Edward was compelled to abdicate in favour of his 14-year-old son, another Edward. He was then taken to Berkeley Castle in Gloucestershire where he was treated with contempt. In the corner of his cell was a pit where the rotting carcasses of animals were thrown in the hope that he would be smothered by the terrible stench.

Still, he survived and his enemies decided to murder him. Armed with a red-hot poker his assassins entered the cell and impaled him from the rear. His piercing screams could be heard echoing outside the castle walls.

An era of chivalry again returned with King Edward III despite the opening episode of his 50-year reign when he tried and executed Roger Mortimer, the ambitious nobleman who had deposed Edward II on his behalf. At the same time he banished Mortimer's mistress — his own mother — to an isolated castle.

Robert the Bruce was now dead and, as the claimants to the Scottish throne squabbled, Edward saw his opportunity to invade. In 1333 Edward won a great victory against the Scots at Halidon Hill. In his armoury was a brand new weapon — the canon. Thereafter the town of Berwick became English although the county of Berwickshire remained Scottish.

Activities north of the border drew Scotland's ally France into the conflict. When Philip VI opened up a southern front by ousting Edward from Gascony in 1337 it signalled the start of the Hundred Years War. There was little genuine purpose to the war, which amounted to a series of skirmishes, except to confirm the reputation of the English bowman as the best in the world.

Right: *Construction first begun in 1083, however it took 168 years to build Ely Cathedral as the rampaging Black Death decimated its workforce. Due to the shortfall in labour the nave and transepts were roofed in wood instead of stone.*

Edward, still harbouring a claim to the French throne through his mother, nevertheless mistrusted French ambition. By now the wool trade was a vital one to England and so was trade with Flanders, where the craft of weaving flourished.

With a victory at sea against the French fleet already behind him, Edward invaded France. Using gunpowder and canon-fire to great effect, he secured a victory at Crecy, near Calais in 1346. One observer revealed that the English archers 'shot their arrows with such force and quickness that it seemed as if it snowed.'

There followed a siege at Calais. The waiting game was eventually won by Edward who demanded six burgers bring him the keys of the town with nooses already around their necks, ready to be hanged. Only when his Queen, Philippa of Hainault, went on bended knee on their behalf did he show mercy.

A peace treaty in 1360 halted the hostilities only temporarily and, bizarrely, the Hundred Years War lasted for a total of 116 years.

Such was King Edward's respect for the legend of King Arthur that he had his own round table constructed during the first years of his reign. He created the Order of the Garter, the highest honour intended for the bravest of his knights. The Order won its name and motto when his cousin Joan dropped her garter at a ball in 1348. Edward picked it up and fastened it to his own leg. To counter the sniggers, he boldly declared: 'Honit soit qui mal y pense' or 'Let he be ashamed who sees evil in it'. Incidentally, Joan — who was wooed but not won by the king — was in love with the steward of the Earl of Salisbury. To be closer to her lover she wed the earl. But when both died she became the bride of the Black Prince.

Also in the time of King Edward III came the creation of the Courts of Quarter Sessions. These were new courts established in 1363 to deal with low grade offences under the stewardship of justices of the peace. These courts remained in existence until 1971.

Edward died from a stroke in 1377. The crown went to Richard — son of the Black Prince and grandson of Edward III — who was just 10 years old.

BLACK DEATH

At home Edward III's subjects faced the ravages of the Black Death. This was the name given to the bubonic plague, a dreadful disease carried by the fleas of rats which stowed away on ships travelling from the east. Its symptoms were hard black spots and tumours under the arms. The breath of one victim was sufficient to infect the next. Once infected, the victim could expect to survive no longer than a few days.

When it struck in 1348 doctors had nothing with which to combat the menace. The population of Bristol was all but wiped out. Thomas of Bradwardine died two days after arriving in London having been consecrated by the pope as Archbishop of Canterbury.

As the epidemic ran its course, it claimed between one fifth and one third of the English population. In Europe it is estimate the disease killed a quarter of the population, some 25 million people. Sporadic outbreaks continued for two centuries, wreaking havoc in the rural economy by slashing the number of available labourers.

At the time, diarist Henry Knighton wrote: 'Everything was low in price because of the fear of death, for very few people took any care of riches or property of any kind. A man could have a horse that had been worth 40 shillings for half a mark (6s 8d — or 33 pence). Sheep and cattle ran at large through the fields and among the crops and there was none to drive them off or herd them; for lack of care they perished in ditches and hedges in incalculable numbers throughout all districts and none knew what to do.

'Believing that the wrath of God had befallen the English, (the Scots) assembled in Selkirk forest with the intention of invading the kingdom, when the fierce mortality overtook them, and in a short time about 5,000 died.'

Below: *A deserted medieval village at Gainsthorpe in Lincolnshire.*

Right: *Aydon Castle in Northumberland is a fine example of a medieval fortified manor house. Virtually unchanged it survived thanks to its conversion to a farmhouse in the 17th century.*

BLACK PRINCE

At the battle of Crecy, the king's son, also called Edward, distinguished himself. A well-meaning knight summoned the king to help the young Edward, who was clad in black armour, only to be told 'Let the boy win his spurs, for I am determined, if it please God, that all the glory of this day shall be given to him and to those into whose care I have entrusted him.'

The Black Prince, as he became known, fought so valiantly that he was knighted on the battlefield. It was there that he picked up three feathers and the motto 'Ich dien' (I serve) from the fallen Prince John, the blind king of Bohemia. Both have remained emblems of the title to this day.

At the end of the encounter, the bodies of 11 princes, 1,200 knights and about 30,000 soldiers lay dead on the ground.

Throughout the Hundred Years War the Black Prince fought with valour and astonishing bravery all over France. Sadly, the Black Prince died the year before his father. From the little we know of him, we can assume he would have instituted a just rule.

Left: *A 15th century fireplace in the upper chamber of the castle at Ashby de la Zouch.*

Below Left: *Ashby de la Zouch Castle was first established in the 12th century but was reconstructed in the 14th century and most of today's remains date from then.*

Right: *Durham's Barnard Castle on the River Tees was built by Bernard de Balliol whose grandson John founded Balliol College at Oxford. His great-grandson was chosen by Edward III to be king of Scotland.*

Below: *Clifford's Tower, York*

Bottom: *At Baconsthorpe Castle in Norfolk there remains the grand gatehouses of a large 15th century fortified manor house.*

Top Left: *Although it existed from Saxon times Bamburgh Castle owes much to Henry III who made many additions, including the impressive, double-towered east gate.*

Far Left: *Dating back to the middle ages, Berry Pomeroy Castle in Devonshire illustrates a typical medieval construction centring on a rectangular courtyard.*

Left: *Medieval fortifications at Berwick Castle proved useless against the fearsome artillery fire of the 16th century. The strategic site received a major overhaul in Elizabethan times but it was mostly destroyed when the railway station was built.*

Right: *Belsay Hall in Northumberland.*

Above: *Fortified in 1385 to repel a threatened French invasion, the efforts made at Bodiam Castle in Sussex were somewhat wasted as England quickly gained control of the Channel.*

Overleaf: *Beeston Castle, perched on the Cheshire plain, was built in the 1220s by Ranulf de Blundeville but soon became crown property and was further fortified by Edward I.*

Above: *Hever Castle, Kent. Begun in the 1270s Hever Castle wasrefortified by Sir John de Cobham in the 1380s and was purchased in 1462 by the father of former Lord Mayor of London, Sir Geoffrey Boleyn whose daughter Anne became Henry VIII's second wife. She was Queen Elizabeth I's mother and was beheaded on 19 May 1536. On Henry VIII's death the castle was given to his widow, Anne of Cleves.*

Left: *John of Gaunt, a son of Edward III, takes credit for the grandeur of Kenilworth Castle. He redesigned the existing castle in the 1370s, transforming it into a magnificent palace.*

Right: *Dunstanburgh Castle was another castle which bears the hallmark of John of Gaunt. So successful were the fortifications added by him in the 1390s that the castle withstood years of Scottish attacks.*

Overleaf: *An aerial view of Kenilworth Castle reveals the scale of improvements embarked upon by John of Gaunt.*

Above: *Leeds Castle, Kent originated in Norman times and was rebuilt by Edward I. However much of what can be seen today is 19th century reconstruction.*

Left: *Old Scotney Castle, Kent. Fears of French attack led wealthy landowners to fortify manors or build castles. So around 1378 the manor house at Scotney was fortified by its owner. Today Old Scotney comprises a 17th century house and some of the original castle.*

Right: *Another frontline castle in the clashes with the Scots – the shell of Pickering Castle in North Yorkshire indicates its glory days.*

Overleaf: *Stokesay Castle, Shropshire, is in fact a fortified manor house, a priceless relic from the medieval era. Its appearance is due mainly to Lawrence de Ludlow who bought it in 1281 and built the hall and top storey of the north tower.*

Above: *When King John stayed at Warkworth Castle in Northumberland in 1216 it was already a strategic stronghold. It remained a royal castle until 1332 when Edward III sold the property to Henry, 2nd Lord Percy of Alnwick.*

Right: *Warwick Castle is another that started life in Norman times – William I built a castle there in 1068 in the 14th century the Earls of Warwick built the structure we see today.*

Left: *After it was stormed by Prince Louis of France during the reign of King John Dover Castle – a key English defence – was rebuilt. Henry III invested in new fortifications, including 'Constable's gate' built in 1227.*

Far Left: *The undercroft of East Wingfield. Once fortified, East Wingfield in Derbyshire boasted a drawbridge, portcullis and gate after being modified by King richard II's Lord Chancellor, Michael de la Pole, in 1384. Yet its earliest use was as a college.*

Bottom Left: *The isolation of Dunstanburgh Castle was intended to protect its owner Thomas, Earl of Lancaster who was in conflict with Edward II. Alas for Thomas he was captured in Yorkshire where he was executed.*

Below: *Much of what remains of Wingfield Manor was put in place in Tudor times. However, the older outer walls and towers are still evident.*

REBELLION AND CIVIL WAR

The rule of King Richard was put to the test when he still only a teenager. As the Black Death had cut the labour supply so drastically the peasant classes felt for the first time a sense of power. When continued high taxes threatened their very existence they put this power to the test.

Wat Tyler led the Peasant's Revolt of 1381 with assistance from a radical priest called John Ball. In his sermons, Ball preached emotively about the woeful inequality of the baronial system. 'My good friends, matters cannot go on well in England until all things shall be in common; when there shall be neither vassals nor lords; when the lords shall be no more masters than ourselves. How ill they behave to us! For what reason do they thus hold us in bondage? Are we not all descended from the same parents, Adam and Eve?'

Peasants known as villeins — those with only limited rights — marched from Kent to London, gathering all the time in numbers. In the capital they burned down John of Gaunt's palace of the Savoy and broke into the Tower of London where they killed several dignitaries, including the Lord Chancellor and the Archbishop of Canterbury. Another victim in London was the wealthy Richard Lyon. He had once been Tyler's master and had beaten him badly. Now Tyler and his followers wrecked a terrible revenge.

It seemed the 14-year-old king was showing similar steel to his father when he rode out to Mile End to meet the peasants. When he asked them what they wanted they replied: 'We wish you to make us free for ever. We wish to be no longer called slaves, nor held in bondage.' Instantly, Richard offered to meet all their demands and granted a pardon to all those who dispersed.

However the leaders of the revolt and some 30,000 followers were not appeased. At a second meeting held at Smithfield, the horse market, on 15 June, Wat Tyler spoke impudently to the King while fingering a sword. He was stabbed by William Walworth, the Lord Mayor of London, who feared the king would die at the hands of the rebel. As Tyler lay dying his followers rose in uproar. The King rode among them shouting 'I will be your leader; follow me'. And they did, until the king's guard broke up the demonstration. A bloody rebellion was undoubtedly averted by his presence of mind. Yet Richard was callously duplicitous. He instantly went back on his word, undid all the fine promises he made to the crowds and saw the remaining leaders hanged.

This shed a more accurate light on Richard — who was so effeminate and fastidious that he introduced the handkerchief to England! His chief pleasures came from gold and jewels. He became deeply unpopular with his nobles with his choice of ministers, particularly when he made merchant's son Michael de la Pole his Lord Chancellor. A rebellion by leading nobles known as the Appellants in 1388 had the majority of Richard's favourites executed.

Above: *The battlefield at Tewkesbury in Gloucestershire was christened 'Bloody Meadow' after the Prince of Wales was killed there on 4 May 1471 and King Henry VI captured and imprisoned.*

Right: *For centuries churches remained the central focus of village life.*

Richard sought revenge and contrived to have two of the rebels, Thomas Mowbray, Duke of Norfolk and Richard's uncle, and his cousin Henry Bolingbroke, Earl of Derby and son of John of Gaunt, banished. While he was abroad, Bolingbroke's father died. The exile meant he lost his inheritance to the greedy King.

Bolingbroke was furious. To his advantage, he accurately forecast the mood of the country and, while Richard was conquering Ireland, mounted an invasion at Ravenspur in Yorkshire — an area which has since been swallowed up by the sea. Bolingbroke won the majority of the nobles around to his cause and when Richard returned he was imprisoned at Flint castle on the Dee estuary. He was forced back to London to abdicate in favour of Bolingbroke in 1399 and was then held prisoner at Pontefract Castle in West Yorkshire. Richard died there in 1400, either of starvation or violence. It was a brutal end to the Plantagenet line.

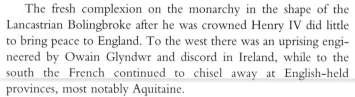

The fresh complexion on the monarchy in the shape of the Lancastrian Bolingbroke after he was crowned Henry IV did little to bring peace to England. To the west there was an uprising engineered by Owain Glyndwr and discord in Ireland, while to the south the French continued to chisel away at English-held provinces, most notably Aquitaine.

Even within his own borders Henry had insurgents with which to contend. The Percy family had once lined up with him. Now they were dissatisfied with his rule and plotted his overthrow. Leading light of the rebel family, which now allied itself with Glyndwr, was Henry Percy — known as Hotspur. On 21 July 1403 Hotspur was killed in the Battle of Shrewsbury by Henry IV and his son Prince Hal, the future Henry V.

Within two years the rebels regrouped. Now the ranks alongside the Earl of Northumberland — father of Hotspur — and Glyndwr were Archbishop Scrope of York and Edmund Mortimer, Earl of March, who had a legitimate claim on the throne as a descendant of Edward III. Henry moved quickly and Scrope was executed, Northumberland killed in the Battle of Bramham Moor in 1408 and the Welsh were slowly but surely subdued.

Like many in the Middle Ages, Henry IV was bewitched by mysticism. When it was foretold that he would die in Jerusalem he prepared to meet his fate by making a pilgrimage to the Holy Land. It was a journey he never found the time to make.

He collapsed in 1413 praying at the tomb of St Edward the Confessor in Westminster Abbey. His dying body was carried into a nearby ante-room decorated with tapestries depicting the story of Jerusalem. It was the Jerusalem chamber, known simply as Jerusalem.

His son, Henry V, who had been at his side in the thick of numerous battles, came to the throne. The truth about this warrior king is much blurred by the Shakespearean legend. Some historians have put a question mark over his reputed wisdom and grace, highlighting his brutality. He thought nothing of putting to death prisoners of war or those who had surrendered on the battle field.

As Prince of Wales he attended the burning of John Badby, a Protestant in the rebel Lollard movement who was convicted of heresy in 1410. After the execution was underway Henry ordered that the flames be doused. In agony Badby was hauled before the Prince and told to recant his beliefs. When he would not the execution continued until Badby's death. Henry would doubtless have justified his cruelty by declaring that it was carried out for the most noble and religiously devout reasons.

It was in pursuit of a claim to the French throne that Henry V arrived on the northern coast of France on 14 August 1415. Having taken Harfleur his forces were severely depleted by an outbreak of dysentery. Accordingly, Henry marched on Calais in order to meet a convoy of ships and return home. The French seized their opportunity to attack. Despite overwhelming odds, Henry and his army won a tremendous victory at Agincourt on 25 October, thanks for the most part to the longbow men of the ranks. Nearly 7,000 French fighters were killed compared to no fewer than 1,000 English fatalities.

Right: *Richard II, the crouch-back king, was defeated and killed at the Battle of Bosworth Field in Leicestershire in 1485.*

Overleaf *The octagonal Dunster Yarn Market is a tribute to the medieval influence in the Somerset town which is overshadowed by a romantic castle.*

Battle observer Jehan de Wavrin, on the French side, wrote afterwards:

'When the battalions of the French were formed, it was grand to see them; and as far as one could judge by the eye, they were in number fully six times as many as the English. And when this was done the French sat down by companies around their banner, waiting the approach of the English and making their peace with one another; and then were laid aside many old aversions conceived long ago; some kissed and embraced each other which it was affecting to witness; so that all quarrels and discords which they had had in time past were changed to great and perfect love . . .

'The said French were so loaded with armour that they could not support themselves or move forward. In the first place they were armed with long coats of steel, reaching to the knees or lower, and very heavy, over the leg harness, and besides plate armour also most of them had hooded helmets; wherefore this weight of armour, with the softness of the wet ground . . . kept them as if immovable so that they could raise their clubs only with great difficulty, and with all these mischiefs there was this, that most of them were troubled with hunger and want of sleep.

'Then the English archers . . . began to send their arrows on the French with great vigour. The said archers were for the most part in their doublets, without armour, their stockings rolled up to their knees, and having hatchets and battle-axes or great swords hanging at their girdles; some were bare-footed and bare-headed, others had caps of boiled leather, and others of osier, covered with harpoy or leather.'

After the battle, fearing a further attack, Henry ordered all prisoners to be killed, wiping out great numbers of French noblemen at a stroke. At home, the triumph did much to distract from domestic tensions. In 1417 Henry returned to France to conquer much of Normandy. By an alliance with the Duke of Burgundy and his betrothal and marriage to Catherine of Valois, daughter of the French King Charles VI, Henry V was declared regent and heir to the throne of France.

This was his aim. Henry felt it his bounden duty to unite England and France. Impressed by his strength and discipline and appalled at the insanity evident in their own shambling monarch, many French people concurred.

The face of Europe might have been much changed had the bold Henry taken this second crown. In fact he died of dysentery while on a soldiering campaign in France. Two months later the French king was himself dead.

Henry's only son was just nine months old when he was proclaimed King of England and, soon afterwards, King of France. The English forces under the leadership of the king's uncle, John, Duke of Bedford, at first maintained a strong foothold in France. However the reversal of fortunes inevitably occurred, in a most romantically sensational way thanks to Joan of Arc.

Henry VI was but a child when the gains his father made in France were lost. He was crowned in Paris in 1430 aged 10 but never returned and would not countenance leading an army there. Few French people took the coronation of the foreign king seriously. Even had he been fully grown, the outcome would probably have remained much the same, for Henry lacked the passion for war that his father and grandfather both had had and he abhorred violence and bloodshed. It was his peaceable nature that earned him the affection of his people and the contempt of his wife Margaret and the warrior nobles.

His interests lay in academia and it was he who founded both Eton College, the exclusive private school near Windsor in Berkshire, in 1440, and King's College, Cambridge, a year later.

Although there were some military successes for the English, France consolidated its strength. The tide turned against the English and by 1453 their cause was utterly lost. It was the same year that Henry VI was struck down by the same madness that blighted his maternal grandfather. Calais was held until 1558 although it was a full 200 years after that before the claim on the French throne by the English monarchy was dropped once and for all.

The loss of possessions in France was a serious blow to English prestige. The murmurings of discontent were finally translated into a fully fledged rebellion by Richard, Duke of York, in 1455. He was descended from the third son of Edward III while Henry VI's claim to the throne was through the fourth son, John of Gaunt, Duke of Lancaster.

The dispute between the two sides was to last 30 long years, and was known as the War of the Roses because of the antagonists' emblems — a red rose for the Lancastrians, a white rose for the Yorkists. The impact of the civil war on ordinary folk was not great, although there were battles in eight counties, with campaigns which in total accounted for about 15 months out of three decades. Worst affected were the noblemen, as it became customary to execute aristocratic prisoners of war in the aftermath of every battle.

Richard, Duke of York, scored an immediate success by forcing the king to accept him as regent. Then a son was born to the ambitious Queen Margaret, nicknamed 'the She-wolf of France'. Now there was an heir to the throne, an unwelcome complication as far as the Yorkists were concerned but a rallying point for the Lancastrians.

When Richard was killed at the Battle of Wakefield, his son Edward assumed leadership of the Yorkist cause. His forces defeated the Lancastrians in a battle fought in blizzard conditions at Towton, in Yorkshire, on 29 March 1461. Henry and his queen escaped to Scotland and plotted a counter-revolt. When the bid to overturn Edward failed in Northumberland, Margaret and the Prince of Wales only narrowly escaped capture. It is said that a vicious robber who then seized them took pity on the queen and her young son, and spared them, not wishing to have royal blood on his hands.

In 1474 the Lancastrians repeated the bid, only to be defeated at Hexham. Margaret and her son fled to France while Henry disguised himself as a beggar and contentedly wandered the hills and dales of Yorkshire until he was recognised and taken to the Tower of London. By then Edward was on the throne.

A switch in allegiance by the powerful Richard Neville, Earl of Warwick, helped to oust Edward in 1470. The earl, whose perpetual power-plays earned him the title 'king-maker', was perturbed by Edward's choice of bride. The handsome king had fallen in love with Elizabeth Woodville, a low-born widow of a Lancastrian stalwart. When Edward began to favour her family above the earl's, Richard Neville changed sides, received aid from King Louis XI of France and placed Henry once more on the throne.

Right: *An artist's impression of strip farming which predominated in the Middle Ages.*

It did not take the exiled Edward long to summon assistance from Charles the Bold, Duke of Burgundy and long-time adversary of Louis XI, and return from Holland with an army which took London in 1471. On a foggy Easter Day, Edward fought a decisive battle at Barnet, in Hertfordshire, in which the Earl of Warwick was slain.

On 4 May the same year, a battle was fought at Tewkesbury in Gloucestershire, at a site which was afterwards christened 'Bloody Meadow'. The Prince of Wales was killed and Henry VI was captured and committed once again to the Tower of London. Within three weeks he was dead. Although the cause of death was officially given as 'pure displeasure and melancholy' he was undoubtedly murdered, probably by Edward's brother Richard, as he prayed in a small chapel in the Tower. Every year, on 21 May, the authorities of Eton school mark the anniversary by placing a wreath of lilies and roses at the spot where he died.

The tussle between the Yorkists and Lancastrians was not over yet, however. Edward IV died prematurely in 1483, his reign perhaps best marked by the construction of St George's Chapel, a fine building at Windsor which he had built to outshine Henry VI's chapel at Eton.

Next in line was his son Edward V, who was just 12 years old. He was king for 77 days before his uncle, Richard, Duke of Gloucester, took the crown. The facts of the coup d'etat are murky. Richard cloaked it as concern for the boy king, however Richard was popular and there was little dissent. It was allegedly with the safety of the young Edward and his 10-year-old brother Richard, Duke of York, in mind that the pair were dispatched to the Tower of London. They were never seen alive again.

It is believed the boys were killed in the Tower of London at a place known ever since as the Bloody Tower. Bones of two children were discovered in the vicinity in 1674 and they were removed and buried in Westminster Abbey. In 1933 examinations of those bones revealed that they belonged to two brothers, aged 12 and 10 and at least one had been suffocated. Later findings had those same bones belonging to younger children who were perhaps girls. In short, nobody knows for sure the fate that befell the little princes.

Theories about the perpetrator and means of their murder are legion. Most popularly accepted is that Richard killed them or had them killed. Having declared himself king, he would have been unwilling to hand over the trappings of rule to his nephew. He never denied being responsible for the murders, even when he was openly accused of them by the French. The princes vanished at a time when Richard carried out a spate of executions to secure his position. Romantics have Sir James Tyrell, a supporter of Richard's, as the murderer. He was apparently a descendant of Walter Tirel, the man thought to have fired the arrow which killed William Rufus back in 1100.

Could the future Henry VII have been responsible for the killing of the little princes? He already had designs on the throne and would, like Richard, have had to make way for the young Edward when he came of age. Supporters of Richard claim the Tudors blackened his name to disguise Henry's complicity in the killings.

Richard was mildly deformed from birth, which earned him the nick-name 'Crouchback'. To call him hunchback would have been too strong a term. He was a disciplined ruler, faced as he was with widespread corruption and intrigue among the noblemen. He was a forceful leader at a time when forceful leadership was needed. But

Above: *The exterior of a typical medieval merchant's house during the age when England began its tradition as 'a nation of shopkeepers'.*

Above Right: *At Ospringe in Kent, Maison Dieu, an ancestor of today's hospitals, looks much the same as it would have done when it was built in the 16th century.*

Below Right: *The 14th century tithe barn in Bradford-on-Avon, Wiltshire, is among the best preserved in the country.*

the string of executions he ordered diminished his popularity. The Duke of Buckingham, once a close aide, opened covert negotiations with Henry Tudor, Earl of Richmond, whose claim to the throne was that he was grandson of Queen Catherine, widow of Henry V and her lover Owen Tudor, and descendant of John of Gaunt.

The traitorous Buckingham was caught and killed but Henry continued his plans to overthrow Richard. In August 1485 he landed at Milford Haven in Wales with an army of mercenaries recruited in Brittany. At Bosworth in Leicestershire the armies clashed. A secret deal struck by Henry with the nobles deprived the king of crucial forces on which he was reliant — Richard was killed and there was victory and a the throne of England for Henry Tudor.

Above: *A rainbow illuminates the dreamy spires of Oxford.*

Left: *Leigh Court Barn is a magnificent 14th century wood-framed barn – the largest of its kind in England – originally intended for the accommodation of monks.*

Right: *Age-old traditions are still observed at Balliol College, Oxford, the home of English academia.*

THE TUDOR AGE

Henry VII was determined to bring peace to his kingdom. He united the Lancastrians and Yorkists by marrying Edward IV's daughter Elizabeth. Diplomatically, he adopted as his emblem a double rose — the famous Tudor rose —blended with white and red, the two colours of the warring houses. There were uprisings to quell, of course, as usurping had become something of a habit in England in previous years.

A usurper who was posing as a nephew of Edward IV and Richard III caused a stir by getting himself crowned Edward VI in Ireland — however he was actually a carpenter's son by the name of Lambert Simnel. In 1487 he attempted an invasion of England. Alas for him, the real nephew was being held in the Tower of London and was duly paraded to prove that Simnel was a hoaxer. Henry must have been amused about the impostor; instead of executing him the king set Simnel to work in the royal kitchens.

Perkin Warbeck was not so fortunate after asserting that he was the younger of the princes in the Tower. With the support of French and Scottish kings, he made several bids to destabilise Henry until he was captured and hanged at Tyburn in 1499.

By his careful management, Henry brought about new prosperity, not least to his own purse. Mindful of waste, he insisted upon checking and initialling every receipt issued by the Treasury. He fostered trade with foreign countries while protecting the domestic market. When he died in 1509 he was a millionaire.

One outstanding problem remained — the succession: his eldest son and heir had already died. Arthur, Prince of Wales, was an important instrument of new European union. He had been betrothed to and subsequently married Catherine of Aragon, the daughter of Ferdinand and Isabella of Spain. On 1 November 1499 when he was 13 years old Arthur wrote her a love letter which began: 'Most illustrious and excellent lady, our dearest betrothed...'

Within five months of the marriage he was dead. Now the sole surviving son would be king. But first there was a dilemma to resolve. Henry VII had been delighted at the political match made by his elder son and decided it was too good an opportunity to waste, not least because of her wealth. It was his intention that the widow should wed again, this time to Henry, the brother of her dead husband. That way the politically valuable union with Spain was maintained and Henry got to keep the huge dowry that Catherine had brought with her.

The problem lay with the church, which opposed a man marrying his dead brother's wife, however, Pope Julius II was persuaded to grant dispensation for the marriage which finally went ahead. Henry succeeded to the throne and married in 1509.

At first he seemed like a breath of fresh air in England which had been yoked by the sobriety of his penny-pinching father. Henry VIII cut a dashing figure when he attended tournaments and banquets adorned in fine clothes. An attempt at invasion by the Scots under James IV was spiked, thanks mostly to the efforts of Queen

Above: *On 9 September 1513 the English forces led by Thomas Howard, Earl of Surrey, defeated the Scots at Flodden Field.*

Right: *It took 14 years to build Dartmouth Castle which was started in 1481. Outstanding not only for its thrilling profile but also because it was the first English castle built specifically to use artillery.*

Catherine who dispatched an army headed by the Earl of Surrey to thrash the intruders at Flodden Field in Northumberland. A short, sharp burst of aggression against France gave way to peace. Enmity between England and France was laid to rest after a meeting near Ardres, northern France. The site was tagged the Field of the Cloth of Gold because of the breath-taking the spectacle of royal regalia.

Henry found plenty of opportunity to pursue his pleasures, including lute-playing, eating and bedding pretty women. On New Year's Day in 1511, to Henry's immense delight, Catherine gave birth to a son. Within seven weeks he died. Four more babies died before one, Princess Mary, survived infancy. Then the affliction of infant mortality returned to haunt Catherine. It was a source of irritation and then anger for the king, who had meanwhile noticed and become besotted with Anne Boleyn, a former lady-in-waiting to his sister Mary.

Troubled by the absence of a male heir, Henry began to convince himself that his marriage to Catherine was wrong in the eyes of God. He sought to disentangle himself, seeking an annulment from Rome. At this stage, Henry was anti-Protestant and happily ensured that so-called heretics were burned in accordance with the

teachings of Rome. A well-worded broadside against the Lutherans who were gathering momentum in Germany had already earned Henry the title of 'Defender of the Faith' from Pope Leo X.

Using his considerable expertise in theology — Henry was trained in the subject having been earmarked as a boy for the post of Archbishop of Canterbury — he aimed to bring the Pope round to his way of thinking. Yet Pope Clement VII was unwilling to help Henry, primarily because the armies of Catherine's nephew Emperor Charles V were on his doorstep.

For five years there was a stand-off between Henry and the Pope. In that time Henry summoned a parliament, the House of Lords, which acted to change the face of the English church. Henry was still reluctant to break off all links with Rome, not through any loyalty to Catherine, his wife of 23 years, but because of an innate mistrust of Protestantism.

His patience ran out in January 1533 when he discovered that Anne Boleyn was pregnant. Optimistic that the unborn child was a boy, Henry employed a tame Archbishop of Canterbury, Thomas Cranmer, to invalidate his marriage. Within days Henry was married to his beloved black-haired Anne, scarcely bothered by the fact that he had once taken her sister as a mistress or that she had a deformed hand with a sixth finger.

To his crushing disappointment, the child was a girl, Elizabeth. It was probably due to this that the relationship between Henry and Anne rapidly cooled. Henry also found his bride to be something of a shrew. Some historians claim Henry was already impotent, although Anne is said to have found her husband in bed with Jane Seymour at Hampton Court Palace.

Duly Anne herself was accused of adultery and sentenced to be burnt alive or beheaded. It was only 'out of kindness' that Henry agreed the sentence could be carried out by sword to spare her the prolonged agony of the stake.

On 19 May 1536 Anne was paraded through the crowds from her prison in the Tower of London to a prominent scaffold con-

structed on Tower Green. Her dark hair was hidden beneath a close fitting cap. White ermine fur lined the grey cape that she wore and a crucifix dangled from the belt of a crimson skirt. She carried a handkerchief and a small, gold-bound prayer book. She prayed and spoke aloud of her innocence and loyalty to the king before she was blindfolded. Now the French swordsman, brought over especially from Calais at Anne's request, pulled his weighty blade from beneath the straw on the platform. While Anne was distracted by his assistant, he struck a single blow. Afterwards, the eyes and mouth of the queen were seen to flutter for some seconds.

The executioner was paid 100 crowns, a considerable amount. As for Henry, he was engaged to Jane Seymour the day after the execution and married her a week later.

Jane Seymour was the woman of Henry's dreams, not least because she provided for him a son and heir. Edward was born in 1537, although the royal joy was muted after complications set in and killed the mother within two weeks. Although it was undoubtedly Jane Seymour who won his heart — it was next to her that he chose to be buried — the grief of his bereavement did not stop him seeking more wives.

With Henry and England now deeply immersed in Protestantism, a match with Germany's Anne of Cleves was made in 1540. When they met, Henry was filled with dread at her plain face, describing her as 'this Flanders mare'. The marriage remained unconsummated and was annulled amicably in the same year,

Within months, Henry had got the matrimonial habit once more, this time choosing the eminently unsuitable Catherine Howard as a wife. Like her cousin Anne Boleyn, Catherine was bored by Henry, mocked his sexual shortcomings and had affairs elsewhere. And like her cousin, she was also convicted of adultery and beheaded. Henry's treatment of his wives revealed a cruel disregard which was evident elsewhere in his reign. Here was the king who introduced the horrible penalty of boiling alive for poisoners.

His sixth and final wife was the amiable Catherine Parr who

married Henry in 1543, four years before he died. Upon his deathbed, Henry's swollen belly measured some 137cm (54in). There has been speculation that some thyroid problem was to blame for his immense girth, yet his gluttony was legendary and was most likely the cause of his incredible bulk.

During the reign of King Henry VIII, the church had changed beyond recognition in England. Henry had the utmost respect for the legislature but had a habit of making laws which suited his own ends. Accordingly, an Act of Parliament was passed which made it treasonable to deny the king's titles. The key title was Supreme Head of the Church of England. Of course, all good Catholics believed the Pope was the indisputable head of the church. A further act required an oath to be sworn throughout the kingdom. Accompanied as it was by vast amounts of pro-Henry propaganda, many people took the oath with varying degrees of enthusiasm.

Those who refused, most notably his Chancellor, Sir Thomas More, and John Fisher, Bishop of Rochester, paid with their lives. The abbot and monks of the Charterhouse in London refused to take the oath and were hanged, drawn and quartered. Henry's first wife Catherine and their staunchly Catholic daughter Mary were placed under house arrest when they would not take the oath. Catherine died in 1536 and Mary, against her better judgment, relented and voiced the necessary vow.

Until this time, monasteries and abbeys had flourished in England. Many of the fundamental monastic virtues like poverty and chastity had long since disappeared, and many monks and priests had been amassing sizable fortunes for years while they indulged in sexual pleasures. Yet these were generalisations. At the same time there were plenty of monasteries providing a haven to the poor, and also food and education to the needy. They were a place of safety from which no one was turned away.

Henry wanted the church to fall into rank behind him, having broken all relationships with Rome. He sent out inspectors to scrutinise the religious institutions. The inspectors did not have to look too far to find misuse and abuse of monasteries and they furnished Henry with the evidence he was seeking. They reported: 'Manifest sin, vicious carnal and abominable living is daily used and committed amongst the little and small abbeys.' Another report described the Abbot of Langdon as: 'The drunkenest knave living. All his canons be even as he is, not one spark of virtue amongst them; arrant bawdy knaves every man.'

In response to reports like these came The Suppression Act of 1536 which effectively dissolved much of the old-style church to make way for the new Church of England. Property and treasures were swallowed up by the state, although the ousted abbots and abbesses were allocated a pension. Monks and nuns were compelled to join the few remaining large houses. Many of the grand Catholic buildings fell empty and crumbled into disrepair. Curiously, ardent Protestants were still being burned in the midst of this anti-Catholic fervour. It is a measure of Henry's tyranny that objections to this wholesale religious change in the church were both small-scale and piecemeal.

There were other positive aspects to his 38-year reign, the

Right: When the combined powers of France and the Holy Roman Empire threatened invasion in 1539, the English replied by building Deal Castle on the exposed Kent coast.

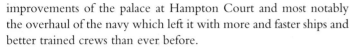

improvements of the palace at Hampton Court and most notably the overhaul of the navy which left it with more and faster ships and better trained crews than ever before.

In 1535 it had been said that God's judgment would fall on Henry after his split with Rome and 'that the dogs would like his blood as they had done Ahab's'. And en route to St George's Chapel, Windsor, as his body lay at Syon Abbey — later to become Syon House — the coffin mysteriously fell open and the next day dogs were found mauling his remains.

His only legitimate son, Edward VI, was just nine years old, a sickly child and as likely to listen to his nurse Sibel Penn, known as Mother Jack, as he was to the Lord Protector, the Duke of Somerset. This duke was Edward Seymour, nominated by Henry because he was brother to the dead queen Jane. Somerset and his colleague Thomas Cranmer, Archbishop of Canterbury, continued the religious reform. Together they produced the *Book of Common Prayer*, significantly entirely in English instead of Latin. Somerset was duly ousted by the ambitious John Dudley, Earl of Warwick and later the Duke of Northumberland, who implemented the more radical *Second Book of Common Prayer*. This was the era of the Protestant nobles and the purists were appalled to see them behaving much as the Catholics had in terms of greed and exploitation.

Edward was every bit as zealous about Protestantism as his noblemen, although his beliefs were more pure and less borne of self-interest. He had to be a key figure if England was to continue down the road to Protestantism. To the alarm of the nobles, the frail Edward contracted consumption and died before his 16th birthday.

Next in line to the throne was Mary, Henry's first daughter and a dogmatic Catholic. Greatly perturbed, Dudley had plotted for a usurper to take the throne. He alighted on Lady Jane Grey, the daughter of the Protestant Duke of Suffolk, who had recently married his son Dudley. The plan even won the support of the king as he lay dying. Jane was a great-niece to Henry VIII but her claim to the throne was further removed than both Mary's and his other daughter Elizabeth. Jane was unwilling to embark upon state treachery but was shamefully manipulated by her ambitious father-in-law.

None had bargained for the national uproar. Mary — for perhaps the only time in her life — was the focus of popular support. Jane, crowned at Syon House, ruled for just nine days before the leading players in the coup were compelled to admit defeat. Mary was proclaimed queen of England by the Lord Mayor of London on 19 July 1553.

At first Jane and her husband, along with Archbishop Cranmer, were spared by Mary who avenged herself with a modest three deaths after coming to power. However, following a Protestant revolt in 1554, Mary decided Jane had to die.

The death of the beautiful, learned 17-year-old Jane, who was beheaded on Tower Green, sparked off a chain of anti-Protestant repression. The Archbishop of Canterbury, Thomas Cranmer was burnt at the stake as a heretic. In prison he recanted against Protestantism no less than eight times but went to his death affirming his beliefs, claiming he had denied his true faith 'for fear of death, and to save my life'. At the stake he thrust forward the hand which had offended by writing such untruths so it would be the first part of his body to be punished.

Mary sought to strengthen the newly returned grip of Catholicism on the country and secure the Catholic succession by marrying Philip, Prince of Spain, a devout guardian of the faith. When the marriage took place in Winchester Cathedral on 25 July

Above: *Hurst Castle was also built in response to a threat of French invasion as part of a chain of forts along the Solent.*

Above Right: *The brick-built Kirby Muxloe Castle in Leicestershire was never completed. Its owner Lord Hastings, a Yorkist, was executed by Richard III for treason.*

Far Right: *Pendennis Castle in Falmouth, with its tall circular tower and 16-sided walls, was one of many defensive forts built by Henry VIII.*

Below Right: *Portland Castle in Dorset and its pair Sandsfoot, which stands opposite, were fortifications ordered by Henry VIII, convinced that war with the French was imminent.*

1554 Philip became King of England, although he was rarely on the shores of his adopted land.

The burning of heretics was unremitting and earned the queen the title of 'Bloody Mary'. English people, who so disliked foreigners, saw their kinsmen being slaughtered at the stake on behalf of the Pope in Rome and a Spanish king.

Meanwhile, war was provoked with France, where its ruler King Henry II was fearful over the unification of his two time-honoured enemies, England and Spain. England was defeated and thrown out of its last remaining French possession, Calais.

This was a humiliating body-blow to Mary who was already grieving at the prolonged absences of her husband on affairs of state. (In truth Philip had quickly wearied of the dour, devout Mary and willingly stayed away.) A few days before her death she told her ladies-in-waiting: 'When I am dead and opened you will find Calais lying in my heart.'

Above: *Walmer Castle is another fortification inspired by Henry VIII out of fear of the French. It was built along a stretch of coast in Kent along with Deal and Sandown Castles. Its main purpose was to aim artillery seaward at an approaching enemy.*

Right: *Buildwas Abbey in Shropshire was founded in 1135. It was run by an order of Cistercian monks from 1147 until its dissolution by King Henry VIII.*

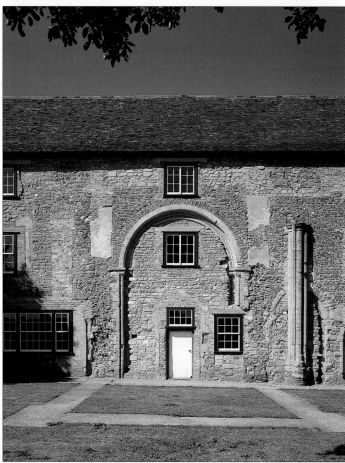

Top Left: *Among the religious houses dissolved during the reign of Henry VIII was the Benedictine priory at Binham in Norfolk.*

Left: *Founded in the 12th century Denny Abbey in Cambridgeshire was in 1342 taken over by Mary de St Pol, Countess of Pembroke and the founder of Pembroke College, Cambridge. The Franciscan nunnery she established existed until the Dissolution.*

Above: *Easby Abbey survived the centuries because, following its dissolution, it was used as a granary.*

Top Right: *Egglestone Abbey at sunset – the splendour of the Abbey, which stands on the River Tees, before it fell to ruin is apparent.*

Right: *Transepts, the chancel and the east side of the cloisters at Furness Abbey in Cumbria are remarkably well preserved.*

Far Left: *The west tower of Furness Abbey, which was begun in 1500, was never completed. By 1537 the Abbey had been dissolved.*

Above Left: *Although the church at Haughmond Abbey in Shropshire was pulled down, the abbot's chamber and hall is remarkably well preserved. After Dissolution the site became a squire's home.*

Left: *During the Dissolution the abbot and one monk at Jervaulx Abbey in Leyburn, North Yorkshire, were executed and the church was blown up. Its stonework was carried away for use elsewhere.*

Above: *The secluded limestone valley which is home to Roche Abbey in Yorkshire was landscaped by Capability Brown in the late 18th century.*

Right: *Kirkham Priory, founded in 1110, was once prosperous thanks to the patronage of local nobility. Now only fragments of the Yorkshire priory remain.*

Left: From the Chapter House at Westminster Abbey a mural telling the story of St John.

Below: A reconstruction of St Augustine's Abbey shows how grand religious houses had become in early Tudor times.

Right: The tiled floor of the Chapter House at Westminster Abbey is rich in detail.

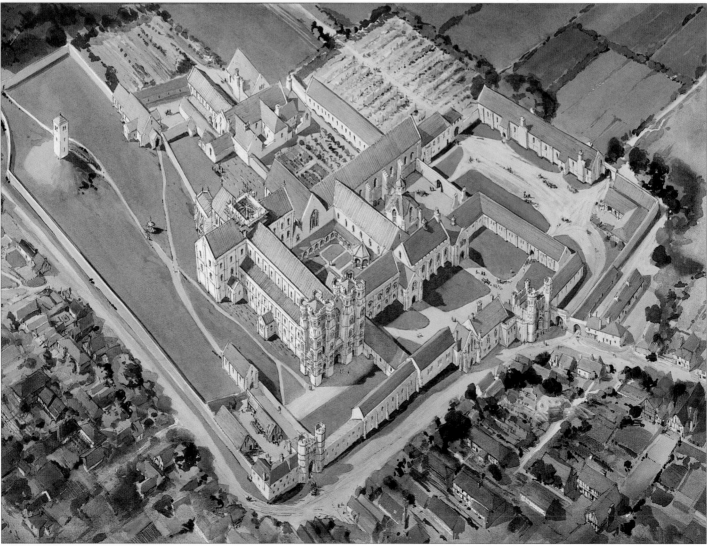

GOOD QUEEN BESS

At the death of Mary, beacons of celebration were lit around the countryside and there was joy at the succession of the Protestant Elizabeth. The optimism of the people of England was well-placed.

Elizabeth, who was born at Greenwich in 1533 but grew up at Hatfield House, Hertfordshire, had witnessed the country swing from zealous Protestantism to rabid Catholicism but had declined to become involved in intrigue. Instead she spent her time in study, distinguishing herself as a musician. She spoke French, Spanish and Italian and had a good grasp of the classics. Thanks to her taste for poetry, an era of fine verse was ushered in.

Elizabeth rode to London at her half-sister Mary's side when the rebellion with Lady Jane Grey as its figurehead collapsed. While Elizabeth shared the religious beliefs of the usurpers she had youthfully strong principles regarding the sanctity of the royals and 'Sacred Majesty'.

She got a taste of what plotting might bring when she was imprisoned in the Tower of London because of an alleged involvement with a rebellion again Mary. Outraged, she refused to enter the palatial prison by Traitor's Gate. Instead, she sat herself on a rock protruding from the Thames riverbed and declared: 'Better sit here than in a worse place.' One of the ramparts at the Tower where the future queen was fond of exercising is still called Elizabeth's Walk.

She was sitting under an oak tree in the grounds of Hatfield House when she first learned that she had succeeded to the throne. She held her first council in the Great Hall there, now the only remaining part of the house which Elizabeth knew so well. The rest was rebuilt in a subsequent century.

Her position was, on the face of it, a tricky one. Here was the product of the liaison between Henry and Anne Boleyn — which had caused the fissure of the national faith in the first place — taking the throne. Catholics at home and abroad believed her illegitimate. And she was ruling a country that had been brow-beaten by the intense religious persecution inspired by Mary.

With the counsel of her most trusted advisor, the able William Cecil (later Lord Burghley), Elizabeth chose a wise path. She set about national meet-the-people tours which evoked a fresh unity of purpose. Instead of seeking retribution for the Protestants martyred by Mary, she accepted that judges and the like had been merely following orders. If they once again followed orders and accepted the ethics of Protestantism, none would be harmed. The Bishop of London, 'Bloody' Bonner, and Nicholas Harpsfield, the archdeacon of Canterbury, refused to accept the edict and were thrown into jail. As they were deeply implicated in the burning of Protestants, the move delighted many people. The celebration of Mass was banned; yet those who pursued the Catholic religion behind closed doors were for the most part left alone.

In 1563 a book compiled by the Protestant scholar John Foxe helped to establish Protestantism more firmly in England than any-

SHAKESPEARE

Few Englishmen have made as much impact on the world as playwright William Shakespeare. The giant of English literature, he was born in the opening years of Elizabeth's reign and produced his first plays before her death. He was the son of a merchant who became the mayor, and went to grammar school in his home town of Stratford Upon Avon where he married Anne Hathaway. In his twenties the lure of the stage drew Shakespeare to London. He became an actor with the Lord Chamberlain's Company of players, later to become the King's Company. After he graduated to writing plays, his first works, produced after 1589, were *Henry VI*, *Richard III* and *The Comedy of Errors*. Although he bought New Place, a large house in Stratford, he stayed mostly in London, absorbed as he was with productions at the Globe Theatre in Southwark which he partly owned. His last play *The Tempest* was penned in 1611 before he retired to Stratford. He died in 1616, leaving an indelible mark on not only English but world theatre.

Right: *Hampton Court was a favourite residence of Henry VIII who jealously purloined the palace from Cardinal Wolsey in 1528. His daughters — Queen Mary and Queen Elizabeth — both used Hampton Court extensively: it was there that Mary waited in vain for Philip of Spain's child. Elizabeth was kept captive here for much of Mary's reign but must have liked the palace for she continued to spend Christmas there each year.*

thing that had gone before. In an astonishing four million words, the *Book of Martyrs* related the suffering of Protestants both at home and abroad, swaying the sympathies of many who were hitherto unconvinced about the new faith. The book, reproduced in 1570, was as widely read as the *Bible*. Not only did it bring waverers into the Protestant fold but it also engendered a deep hatred and mistrust of Catholicism and the papists.

Elizabeth was determined to preserve a moderate Protestant England. Even though she embraced the new faith, she disliked its more radical aspects, like the abolition of bishops, which was being called for by the Calvinists of Geneva.

Walking this fine line, she politely declined numerous marital matches with foreign crowned heads, Catholic and Protestant alike. Her true love appears to have been Robert Dudley, Earl of Leicester, who wooed her for 19 romantic days in Kenilworth

Castle in July 1575. Even now her sense of duty prevailed. The courtship was never formalised. With his wife dying in suspicious circumstances shortly before the affair got underway, a scandal would have ensued and would have dented the prestige of the flame-haired royal.

The most pressing problem thrown up by the religious divide was that of Mary, Queen of Scots. Mary was the Catholic daughter of James V of Scotland and the French noblewoman Mary of Guise. She was also a great niece of Henry VIII which gave her a claim on the English throne. Elizabeth may have been uncomfortable in this knowledge but she was not half as concerned as her closest advisors. For if Elizabeth died, the crown would go to Mary. And while Mary lived, there was every chance of a Catholic assassination attempt on Elizabeth so that England would be restored to popery.

After growing up in France, Mary married the heir to the French throne, Francis. Following his death in 1561, she returned to Scotland and, at the age of 22, wed her cousin, the 19-year-old Lord Darnley. Six years later he was murdered and she married for the third time. This time her groom was the Earl of Bothwell, the man thought to be Darnley's killer.

Scotland was divided in its support between Mary and her son, James (who later became James I, the first Stuart king of England). There was keen suspicion that she was involved in the killing of Darnley. Many of the nobles were now Protestant. It was the Protestants who eventually imprisoned Mary on an island in Loch Leven in Scotland where she was forced to abdicate in favour of James.

Mary was ultimately exiled from Scotland and fled to England.

She expected asylum from Queen Elizabeth who was undoubtedly sympathetic to her plight. However, her very existence posed a threat to the English queen. Even if Mary herself did not propose to harm her, she became the focus of plots against the monarch. Elizabeth at first used Mary to control the Catholics of Scotland. She could not find the enthusiasm to have her killed; if nothing else, the authority of the crown would be severely weakened by such a regicide. Only when dubious evidence was produced by spies of the duplicitous Sir Francis Walsingham that Mary had twice plotted against the queen, did a treason trial take place.

Mary was convicted some 19 years after arriving in England and, albeit reluctantly, Elizabeth signed the execution warrant. Afterwards the English queen claimed she did not send off the vital document but that an under-secretary of state had dispatched it without telling her. The official was jailed for two years.

The execution took place indoors on 15 February 1586 in the Great Hall of Fotheringhay Castle, near Peterborough. When the executioners asked for forgiveness, Mary told them: 'I forgive you with all my heart, for now, I hope, you shall make an end of all my troubles.' With a serene smile, she prepared herself for death. Her ladies-in-waiting removed religious jewellery from her neck and her top clothes until she was stripped to a fulsome petticoat. Her loyal attendants could not bear the torment and broke down into tears. Mary soothed them with words spoken in French, embracing each one in turn. Before they withdrew, one pinned a cloth across her face.

There were no signs of fear as the Scottish queen knelt on a cushion and quoted a psalm in Latin before laying her head on the block. The executioner must have been overcome with awe for the first blow of the axe only succeeded in knocking her senseless and it took three swings to completely sever her head. Afterwards he held up the head and cried: 'God save the Queen.' Observers saw her lips move for some 15 minutes after the impact of the axe.

Only after the deed had been carried out did the executioner find her small, faithful dog hiding in her petticoats. The hound's hairy coat turned red with blood as it sat between his mistress's head and shoulders, snapping at those trying to retrieve him.

Mary's death outraged the rest of Europe. Elizabeth had long benefited from the politics of hate which existed between France and Spain. Neither acted against England because each was too concerned with the activities of the other.

Elizabeth and her navy had been aggravating the Spanish with attacks on the motherland and the colonies. Now Philip of Spain decided to move against England. He gathered a mighty Armada with the aim of obliterating the English navy and then invading. An early blow to his plan came when Sir Francis Drake sailed into Cadiz harbour in 1587 and let rip into the flotilla of galleons, causing massive damage.

Not until the 15 July 1588 did the Armada, with its 8,000 sailors and 18,000 soldiers, reach the English Channel heading for Calais. As legend has it, Drake was playing bowls on Plymouth Hoe when the Spanish ships were sighted and he insisted on completing the game before setting sail. Small English ships, stealthy and swift, harried the Armada in the Channel. Then Drake once again inflicted serious damage by sending fire-ships into Calais harbour.

The invasion plans were shelved but further tragedy was to come for the Spanish. As they headed back out to sea, gales devastated the remainder of the fleet. Only a few escaped by sailing around the top of Scotland and returning to Spain via Ireland.

It was to her troops at Tilbury on 8 August that Elizabeth famously said: 'I have the body of a weak and feeble woman but I have the heart and the stomach of a king, and of a king of England too.' Even as she spoke, the menace of the Armada had been destroyed. Afterwards she had a medal struck inscribed with the words 'Deus flavit, et dissipati sunt', meaning 'God blew, and they were scattered'.

Elizabeth died on a bed of cushions at Richmond Palace in Surrey in her seventieth year. The body of Good Queen Bess lies in the same tomb as her sister Mary in Westminster Abbey.

Above: *At Tilbury Fort Elizabeth I assured her troops: 'I have the body of a weak and feeble woman but I have the heart and the stomach of a king, and a king of England, too.'*

Below: *Queen Elizabeth's Pocket Pistol at Dover Castle, the fort which was a vital Channel defence.*

Above Right: *Although it has been abandoned since the beginning of the 19th century, the local limestone of Kirby Hall in Northamptonshire has weathered the years well and still evokes a picture of Elizabethan grandeur.*

Below Right: *Sir Thomas Pomeroy was lord of Berry Pomeroy Castle until 1549 when he refused to give up Catholicism. As he fell from grace his lands were snapped up by Edward Seymour, Duke of Somerset, a leading proponent of the new faith under the Protestant King Edward VI.*

REGICIDE AND RESTORATION

At the death of Elizabeth, a horseman galloped from London to Edinburgh in 60 hours to inform the heir to the throne, James VI of Scotland, that his hour had come. When he made the journey south to London, James marvelled at the wealth of his new kingdom, so apparent in the homes and castles of his noblemen. In Scotland life was much more dour. With his coronation in 1603, he became James I of England, the first of the Stuarts. He returned but once to his native Scotland.

The king declared, like the succession of monarchs who had gone before him, that he was the divinely chosen head of the Church of England. As the son of Mary, Queen of Scots and the murdered Lord Darnley, he was religiously suspect in the eyes of the Protestants. Yet neither was he accepted by the Catholics.

In 1605 a determined group of Catholics led by Robert Catesby and Thomas Percy plotted to blow up the king and members of the House of Lords during the opening of Parliament on 5 November. In the cellars beforehand, a veteran of the Spanish army, Guido Fawkes, was supervising the use of the explosives. He was seized after one of the plotters wrote a letter to a friend warning him not to attend the formalities. The letter was handed straight to the authorities.

Although the use of torture was illegal under England's justice system, Fawkes endured appalling suffering until he named his co-conspirators. They were hanged, drawn and quartered on 31 January 1606. Their activities are still marked annually in England with Fireworks Night on 5 November.

The question mark over state religion continued. Puritans, plain-living Protestants who worked as lawyers, sought to colonise the New World. Catholics took refuge in Spain and France where their religion was strictly observed.

There were other ways in which James lost favour with his people. He was a homosexual who showered rewards on his lover George Villiers, finally elevating him to Duke of Buckingham. Ultimately, Buckingham was killed on 23 August 1620 by an ex-army Lieutenant, John Felton, who claimed he was both owed money and bypassed for promotion. Felton fought his way to the duke through a collection of army personnel to lunge a dagger into him. His victim turned around, uttered the word 'villain' before collapsing. Reflecting the unpopularity of Buckingham in the country, Felton wrote: 'He is unworthy of the name of a Gentleman or Soldier, in my opinion, that is afraid to sacrifice his life for the honour of God, his King and Country.' He was hanged on 27 November 1620.

James inspired a panic about witchcraft which led to mass persecution. He was convinced in the power of the occult, firmly believing that a storm which lashed the ship bringing himself and his 15-year-old bride Queen Anne from Denmark was witches' work. Two women were burned at the stake — one while still alive — after admitting as much. In 1597 he had written *Daemonologie*, all

Above: *This painting from the studio of Sir Anthony Van Dyck, 'The three eldest children of Charles I' hangs in the Ranger's House.*

Right: *Charles I after Cornelius Johnson; this too hangs in the Ranger's House.*

about witches, to counter Reginald Scot's sceptical book *Discoverie of Witchcraft* which appeared in 1583. The superstitious king went on to introduce harsh new laws against witches. Yet he was enough of a scholar to study the legal cases brought against witches and grew to realise that many trials were unsound.

He ended one of the most dubious forms of condemnation, that of denunciation by children, at a time when the courts were prepared to accept any flight of fancy by youngsters as evidence. John Smith of Leicester feigned fits and the vomiting of pins to frame old women for casting spells on him. Nine had already been hanged on his evidence before James I intervened. At the king's behest, the boy was dispatched to the care of the Archbishop of Canterbury. Within weeks he broke down, confessing his tale had been fabricated. No more would the words of children wield so much deadly power.

This act went virtually unnoticed. Alas, the same could not be said for the execution of Sir Walter Raleigh. As a court favourite in the Elizabethan Age, Raleigh had enjoyed royal patronage. But he was suspected of plotting against James who also loathed smoking, the habit introduced by Raleigh to English society after one of his forays to the New World. The king described smoking as:

'Loathsome to the eye, hateful to the nose, harmful to the brain, dangerous to the lungs and in the black stinking fume thereof, nearest resembling the horrible Stygian smoke of the pit that is bottomless.'

Generally well-placed the sentiments may have been, but Raleigh nevertheless did not deserve to die for importing the weed. Raleigh had been condemned to death for treachery in 1603 but lived for 13 peaceful years in the Tower of London from where he wrote his *History of the World*. Perhaps yearning once again for a life of adventure, Raleigh convinced the king he could find gold in Guiana. When he returned empty-handed, having stirred up trouble by attacking a Spanish settlement, Raleigh was executed in Old Palace Yard, Westminster, on 29 October 1618.

James's obsession with a union between England and Spain also severely dented his popularity. Spain was a long-time enemy yet he was determined his son Charles would marry the Infanta, the Spanish princess. To secure the agreement, James was even prepared to pave the way for a return to Catholicism. Parliament was outraged. His dream fell apart when Charles, accompanied by the Duke of Buckingham, visited Spain and behaved rudely towards his hosts.

James, a man whose hands were constantly black because he refused to wash them, was once branded by France's Henry IV as 'the wisest fool in Christendom'. By the time of his death in 1625 he had foolishly sacrificed much of the goodwill won for the crown by Elizabeth.

As the king's eldest son Henry died of typhoid in 1612, it was his second son, Charles, who took the crown. Charles was an art lover who was patron to van Dyck and Rubens. He had built for his wife, Henrietta Maria of France, the fabulous Palladian Queen's House at Greenwich. But his artistic bent was lost on politicians who grew to loathe him.

It was rampant taxation that caused the greatest rub. In 1628 the House of Commons presented Charles with a Petition of Right, aimed at protecting people from royal taxes which did not meet with the approval of Parliament. It also banned martial law and declared that no one could be arrested by the king's order without a named charge. Furious at the challenge to his authority, Charles dissolved Parliament in 1629 and ruled without it for 11 years. During this time, he continued to raise money from taxes which was now, thanks to the Petition of Right, illegal.

Charles was trounced in a war with Scotland in 1639. The following year he was compelled to recall Parliament to secure more funds. The Long Parliament, as it was called because it lasted 20 years, released Charles's enemies and imprisoned his advisors, Sir Thomas Wentworth, Earl of Stafford, and the zealous Archbishop William Laud. Charles was forced to sign the assent needed to execute Stafford, who died at Tower Hill on 12 May 1641. When he tried to avenge the death, Charles met open antipathy in London. He left the capital for Oxford, effectively leaving the city to the Parliamentarians. Now King and Parliament were on a collision course. The result was Civil War.

In essence, the king's supporters were the majority of noblemen and the Catholics. Geographically, the heartland of the king's camp was in Wales, the south-west and the north. They were called Cavaliers, a name derived from the Spanish word 'caballeros' used by their enemies to denote that they were papists.

Followers of Parliament were the crop-haired apprentices, the merchants and a few of the noblemen in the London, the south-east and East Anglia, where support for the anti-royalists was greatest.

Crucially, the country's main ports were in the hands of Parliament.

The first clash was in Warwickshire at Edgehill on 23 October 1642. That battle was indecisive but the Cavaliers had the best of the fighting in that and the following year. In September 1643 the Roundheads attracted the vital support of the Scots. In return the Church of England was by law made Presbyterian.

Oliver Cromwell rose to prominence in the ranks of the Roundheads. A member of the Long Parliament, he achieved brilliance as a military tactician and propagandist. He despaired of the rambling strands of the Parliamentarians and moulded the highly organised New Model Army, which by his order was composed of clean-living Puritans.

When the king's forces were eventually defeated at Naseby, in Northamptonshire, on 14 June 1645, the eventual outcome of the Civil War was certain. Yet still the fighting continued with Charles witnessing for himself a further rout at Rowton Heath, Chester. He finally surrendered himself to the Scottish Army at Newark, Nottinghamshire. For a fat ransom, he was handed over to the Parliamentarians.

There was discord among the Protestant victors, centring on the degree to which the faith should now be followed. Charles made capital out of the grievances, carrying out secret negotiations and hoping to win back the throne. For a while he was imprisoned on the Isle of Wight, in Carisbrooke Castle, to remove him from intrigue. When fresh fighting erupted in May 1648 Charles was roundly blamed and was put on trial for his life. The charge against him was that he was a 'tyrant, traitor, murderer and public enemy of the Commonwealth'.

Charles refused to plead, signifying that he did not recognise the court. There were 78 commissioners at the hearing held in Westminster Hall, many of them unwilling to find against the king. It was thanks to enthusiastic efforts by Cromwell that they were persuaded to return a guilty verdict. Charles lived long enough to see the 'Rump' of the Long Parliament, as it was known, declare itself a republic at the start on 1649.

On 30 January 1649 Charles marched from St James's Palace to the sombre sound of beating drums, steadying himself on a gold cane. The scaffold on the balcony of his palace at Whitehall featured an especially low block, a calculated insult to his dignity. Two executioners were present, both heavily disguised for fear of revenge attacks by Royalists. Dressed in black, they wore masks, false beards and heavy coats to alter their shape. One of them was Richard Brandon, nicknamed 'Young Gregory', and it was he who wielded the axe against King Charles. His assistant was William Lowen.

The king asked the executioners not to swing the axe until he gave a sign. The signal was to be the stretching of his arms. With the aid of the executioner and an attendant bishop, he tucked his long hair beneath a white satin cap and stretched himself on the floor of the scaffold with his neck on the block. A devout man, he began to say prayers. A movement by the executioner momentari-

Above Right: *On 14 June 1645 the fate of Charles I was sealed when his troops were routed by the New Model Army under Fairfax and Cromwell at Naseby, Northamptonshire.*

Right: *Boscobell House, dating from the 16th century, sheltered the future King Charles II after the Battle of Worcester. Charles hid in an oak tree while two Parliamentarian soldiers loitered below.*

ly panicked the king. 'Wait for the sign, wait for the sign!' he called urgently. Moments later he spread his arms. The axe fell and Britain was without a monarch.

It is said Brandon was reluctant to take the life of a king and had to be escorted to the scaffold by armed guards. As payment, he was given £30 in half crowns, an orange spiked with cloves and the king's handkerchief. Not long afterwards he fell ill and died. Many believed 'he died of remorse at killing a king'.

Although hundreds attended the execution, the atmosphere was muted. Most felt the forebodings of a national disaster. One bystander was 17-year-old Philip Henry, who wrote: 'The blow I saw given and can truly say with a sad heart at the instant whereof, I remember well, there was such a groan by the thousands then present as I never heard before and desire I may never hear again.'

In 1813 the coffin of Charles I was exhumed from a vault at St George's Chapel, Windsor. Observer Sir Henry Halford cut off a lock of the dead king's hair and removed a vertebra, which he used as a salt cellar on his dinner table. Only when a furious Queen Victoria heard of it some 30 years later was the section of backbone reunited with the body.

The king's execution diminished support for Cromwell, whose so-called 'Commonwealth' further became unpopular through a Puritanical ban on theatre and May fairs. His insistence on religious toleration for Protestant sects infuriated the Presbyterians who considered themselves to have the only acceptable faith. Consequently, the Scots backed the Prince of Wales, who was in exile in Holland, and on 1 January 1651 had him crowned Charles II. However, a bid to install Charles on the English throne was smashed when Cromwell fought the Scots and remaining Cavaliers at Worcester on 3 September 1651.

The adventures of Charles II thereafter became legendary. He is said to have hidden in a oak tree in the grounds of Boscobel House, in Shropshire, while Commonwealth soldiers gossiped below. Dressed as a woman, he finally arrived at Shoreham in Sussex, and set sail for France in a coal brig by the name of *Surprise*.

History puts Cromwell in a bad light given his vicious repression of the Catholics in Ireland and the dreary existence he inflicted on the English. While he was undoubtedly flawed by his bigotry against Catholics, he was in fact highly-principled and strongly motivated. Until his death on 3 September 1658, Cromwell continued to wrestle with the dilemmas thrown up by bickering colleagues. He became so frustrated with the fellows of his party that he dissolved Parliament and made himself Lord Protector. His son Richard briefly held the title until he was overthrown by army generals in April 1659. Disputes continued until Parliament voted to restore Charles II to power.

When Charles entered London on 29 May 1660, the streets were lined with cheering supporters. Charles was a handsome, intelligent bon viveur who loved theatre, horse racing and women. Among his mistresses was Nell Gwyn, an orange seller turned actress, who caught the roving eye of the king. Honest and true, Nell became a folk heroine. When her carriage was mistaken for one carrying another of the king's Catholic lovers and stoned by a mob, she popped her head out of the window and bellowed: 'Don't hurt me, good people! I'm the Protestant whore.' The dying words of Charles to his brother James were reputedly: 'Let not poor Nelly starve.'

The atmosphere of paranoia between the two main religions during Charles's reign culminated in the 'Popish Plot'. Protestant

Above: *On top of a rocky outcrop in the Isles of Scilly, Cromwell ordered the construction of a defensive castle.*

Right: *Portrait of Oliver Cromwell, Lord Protector and signatory to the death warrant of King Charles I.*

Far Right: *Built by persecuted Catholic Sir Thomas Tresham in 1593 the Rushton Triangular Lodge symbolises the triple aspects of the Holy Trinity.*

Below: *Lulworth Castle was built as an ostentatious hunting lodge by Thomas Howard in 1607. Badly damaged during the Civil War it was revitalised by rich Londoner Humphrey Weld who bought it in 1643.*

Titus Oates spread a scurrilous rumour that Catholics were planning to assassinate King Charles. Several Catholics were executed on his word while a wave of anti-Catholicism swept the country.

In Parliament the Whigs — a Protestant political group — pressed for an Exclusion Bill which would bar James, the Catholic brother of the king, from taking the throne. Charles refused it and dissolved Parliament, furnished by cash as he was by the King Louis XIV of France. Until he died in 1685 he ruled as a dictator.

The reign of James II opened in 1685 with an invasion by the Duke of Monmouth, the illegitimate son of Charles II and a popular Protestant. Monmouth's inferior forces were crushed by the army at Sedgemoor, Somerset. It was the last battle to take place on English soil.

Afterwards James pursued his Catholic interests vigorously and elevated fellow believers to the highest ranks of government. The outlook got even bleaker for Protestants when his second wife, Mary of Modena, gave birth to a son who would be raised a Catholic and would one day inherit the throne. James' enemies were convinced the child was an impostor who had been smuggled in to the palace in a bed-pan to ensure a Catholic succession.

It was the last straw. A committee of seven eminent Protestants pleaded with William of Orange, the Dutch ruler, to intervene. William was married to Mary, James II's daughter by Anne Hyde, and was himself grandson of Charles I. A north wind brought William and his forces from Holland to Brixham in Devon on 5 November 1688. James soon realised his cause was hopeless and fled to France, hot on the heels of his wife and son.

There was no armed resistance to William and Mary so the 'Glorious Revolution', as it was known, was gratifyingly bloodless. However, an attempt by James and his supporters, the Jacobites, to win back the English crown was fought out on Irish soil and was

decided in William's favour at the Battle of the Boyne on 1 July 1690. The harsh penalties imposed subsequently on the Irish Catholics who fought for James have scarred Ireland to this very day.

Asthmatic William escaped the city smog by having Kensington Palace built for him by Sir Christopher Wren, the architect who designed London's St Paul's Cathedral. Wren also redesigned much of Hampton Court for William and Mary. William outlived his wife but died in 1702 after a riding accident in the grounds of Hampton Court when his horse stumbled in a molehill and threw him.

Queen Anne, Mary's sister, was his successor. Parliament passed the Act of Settlement in 1701 to ensure a Protestant would always take the throne. For her survival, Queen Anne had to thank the soldierly skills of the Duke of Marlborough. His prowess in the field ensured a clutch of victories against the French King Louis XIV, who was backing James Stuart, the 'Old Pretender', for the English throne. Only after the Treaty of Utrecht in 1713 did Louis XIV withdraw his support for James and recognise Queen Anne as rightful ruler of England.

Queen Anne suffered 10 miscarriages. Unable to provide a successor, the crown would go to Germany, to the Hanoverian offspring of a granddaughter of James I. The colourless Queen Anne died in 1714, bringing to a close one of the most vivid eras of English history.

However, the foundations had been laid for a new age — the future 'glory years' of industrial might and empire. England's ancient history was at an end. Her centuries of prosperous nationhood and world power were dawning. The fledgling born out of the migrant waves of prehistory was about to spread her wings . . .

THE 18TH CENTURY AND BEYOND

Left: *Religious intolerance was one of the themes of English history during the years after the reformation. Hatred for the papacy and catholicism was followed by the bigotry of the rigid nonconformists. In the grounds of Lulworth Castle lies the first Catholic church built in England since the Reformation. Started in 1786, owner Thomas Weld was only allowed St Mary's if it didn't take on the appearance of a church.*

Above: *The great houses of the 18th century sat in a landscape that, while man-made, was softer and more rural than the formal gardens of before. Chatsworth's were designed by Capability Brown who produced the beautiful parkland we see today.*

Right: *The remains of Old Gorhambury House, in Hertfordshire, illustrate the influence of the Renaissance in Elizabethan England.*

Above: *Hampton Court remained untouched from its completion by Cardinal Wolsey for more than 150 years until the reign of William and Mary. They asked Sir Christopher Wren to comprehensively redesign the palace. His initial plans were dropped as being too expensive but the frontage was changed and the gardens laid to a French style which has been recreated today.*

Left: *Ranger's House is a brick villa built in the early 18th century by Admiral Francis Hosier between Greenwich and Blackheath in London.*

Right: *Extensions were made to Ranger's House during subsequent centuries but it remains in essence a typically Stuart house, with its lofty ceilings and orange brickwork.*

Overleaf: *The splendid grand conservatory at Syon House which has been home to the Dukes of Northumberland for more than 200 years.*

Above: *The first building on the site of Syon House was a nunnery founded by Henry V. It owes its interiors today to Robert Adam, the famous designer commissioned by the Duke of Northumberland in 1769 to remodel his new home.*

Previous Page: *Ironmaster Thomas Foley bought the Jacobean mansion Witley Court near Worcester after the Civil War and added two towers. In 1735 the lavishly baroque parish church was added by another member of the dynasty, the 1st Lord Foley.*